THE RIVER STOUR

THE RIVER STOUR

An East Anglian river and its people

by

RUSSELL EDWARDS

TERENCE DALTON LIMITED
LAVENHAM . SUFFOLK

1982

Published by
TERENCE DALTON LIMITED

ISBN 0 900963 34 4

First edition 1982
Reprinted 1988

Text photoset in 11/12 pt. Baskerville

Printed in Great Britain at
The Lavenham Press Limited, Lavenham, Suffolk

© Russell Edwards 1982

Contents

Index of Illustrations

All the photographs were taken by the author.

To
My dog Honey, my constant companion while writing this book, who like Constable loved "every tree, stump and stile."

Acknowledgements

I AM most grateful to the following publishers for permission to use quotations from their books:
Council of the Society for Psychical Research for the quotation from Dr Dingwall's book, *The Haunting of Borley Rectory*. Pitman Books Ltd for the quotations by Sir Alfred Munnings taken from his autobiographies. William Heinemann Ltd for the quotation by Sir Alfred Munnings taken from *The Englishman* by R. Pound. Blackie and Son Ltd for a quotation from *Suffolk Scene*, by Julian Tennyson. Cambridge University Press for the description of Mistley from the translation by Marchand of De la Rochefoucauld's book, *A Frenchman in England*.

I am indebted to the National Trust for permission to photograph the interior of Melford Hall and to Sir Richard Hyde Parker for his help with the narrative concerning Melford Hall. My thanks to Len Head for providing the chapter about fishing the river and to Lady Sue Ryder for her help with the manuscript concerning the Sue Ryder Foundation.

I am also grateful to the following specialists who have contributed towards this book: John Marriage (Stour navigation), Basil Ambrose (Vintner), Kenneth Bird (Restoration of old houses), Patrick Phillips (Kentwell Hall), George Burnett (Bush Boake Allen), Roger and Cheryl Clark (heavy horses), David Randall (orchids), Peter Minter (brick maker), Iain Grahame (World Pheasant Association), the Misses Sylvia and Margaret Richardson, Mrs Kathleen Loe and Miss Hilda Green for their personal recollections of their friend Sir Alfred Munnings, and Bob Pritchard, EDME (malting).

My thanks also to the ladies of the Suffolk Record Office, Ipswich, and finally to both John Venmore-Rowland and Robert Malster for their help with the manuscript.

CHAPTER ONE

Introduction

JOHN Constable, England's greatest landscape painter, and I have just two things in common. During our respective lifetimes our talents have gone unrecognised and unrewarded, producing recurring, impecunious predicaments, but we both have had the privilege of residing in England's most beautiful valley, the Stour, which for most of its eighty-mile course separates Suffolk from Essex.

Constable immortalised this scenery in his paintings; I humbly set out to record in this book stories about the people who have come here throughout the ages, made their homes in it, and have left behind as lasting memorials to their industry the picturesque towns and villages which this book portrays.

About 8000 B.C. the formation of the North Sea separated Britain from the continent and our islands took on roughly the shape that they have today. From this time onwards East Anglia has received migrants from Europe; warriors, farmers and refugees from political and religious persecution, all of whom have woven the tapestry of our river's heritage.

Although the sandy gravel area of the Stour valley was settled very early by prehistoric man, there is very little evidence remaining of his existence. The Bell-Beaker people, Neolithic farmers, came here from Holland more than three thousand years ago* and became the first people to farm the valley. At Brantham Hall, which overlooks the head of the estuary, pottery has been found which belonged to this culture; it is now in the Ipswich museum.

Belonging to the same period in history is the unexcavated site of the henge monument discovered by aerial photography at Stratford St Mary. It is a circular single-entranced ditched and banked ritual structure of the same type as Stonehenge, and is probably the earliest evidence of religious activity in this part of Suffolk.

Following the Bronze Age, the first of the Iron Age settlers came from Southern Holland and Eastern Belgium about 500 B.C. As well as introducing the art of smelting and working iron, they also learnt to improve the keeping qualities of their grain by drying it in clay ovens. One of these ovens has been found in Stutton village.

The next wave of iron age invaders were the militant Marnians, who settled north of the river and were the ancestors of the Iceni tribe of Celts of whom Boudica was the most famous. The Celtic tribe of Trinovantes,

*Carbon dating now puts this date further back to 3400 B.C.

◀ The estuary of the Stour.

descendants of the first Iron Age settlers, occupied the Stour valley and had their capital near Colchester. It was the Marnians who introduced to Britain chariot warfare, which was to be used later by Boudica when she crossed the Stour, probably near Stratford St Mary, on her way to sack Camulodunum (Colchester). When a detachment of the Ninth Legion set out from Lincoln to relieve the garrison, Boudica sent a detachment of her forces scurrying through the Stour valley to defeat the Romans somewhere at the head of the valley, possibly near Wormingford, between Sudbury and Colchester.

The last wave of Iron Age invaders were the Belgic tribes from eastern France and the Belgian Ardennes. They settled in Kent and South Essex and gradually worked their way north to the Stour valley. The great earthwork fortress at Clare, the outline of which is still evident today, may have been used by the resident Trinovantes to resist this Belgic invasion. The successful Belgae (mainly the Catuvellauni tribe, who occupied Essex and an area to the west) were farmers as well as warriors and they settled and farmed the Stour valley. Evidence for their presence comes from wheel-made pottery and cremation cemeteries found at Boxford and a hoard of gold coins belonging to the Gaulish tribe, Atrebates, and dating from 100-75 B.C., discovered at Haverhill.

Apart from the remains of a Roman building beneath the pews of Kedington church and Roman roads at Long Melford, very little remains to remind us of the Roman occupation of the Stour valley. The final days of the Roman occupation witnessed the arrival of the English; the Angles, Saxons, Vikings and the Danes.

King Edmund was crowned king of the East Angles on Christmas day, A.D. 855, on a hillside overlooking the Stour at Bures, the traditional place of the coronation being marked by a small thatched chapel. The first major English naval victory was achieved at the mouth of the Stour off Bloody Point at Shotley in A.D. 885 when King Alfred's newly formed fleet encountered marauding Danish ships, sixteen of which were taken.

In spite of continuing battles between the Anglo-Saxons and Danes, the population of Suffolk began to rise rapidly from 850 until by the time of the Norman conquest this was the most populated part of England. More land was deforested and farms created to support the needs of the increasing populace, leading to a more established and settled way of life bringing with it increased prosperity.

Harold, who became king of England in January, 1066, and in October that year was defeated by the Normans at Hastings, was created Earl of East Anglia in 1045. His personal administration and headquarters were at East Bergholt, where he held about fifteen hundred acres of land. The court of the Royal manor at Bergholt had jurisdiction over most of the other manors in the

Samford Hundred. Harold built a church on the site of the present church, the first church at Bergholt being nearer the river at Flatford.

The Normans were the last military force to invade and conquer England. Their military efficiency brought stability to the area, and together with the increasing trade with the continent and increasing population, laid the foundation of the industrial expansion and wealth of the Stour valley during the medieval period. A delightful Norman church at Wissington with a typical round chancel arch with zig-zag design stands as a commendation to the architecture of this period.

Whosoever has power holds the key to industrial prosperity; that is a maxim as true today, with the scramble for North Sea oil, as it has been throughout history. The Stour was a fast-moving river, until parts of its course were altered to make it more suitable for navigation and locks and sluices were built along its length. The river provided the power to drive watermills to grind corn and for the process of fulling, required in the felting and thickening

A flock of brent geese over the Stour estuary at Holbrook.

Lavenham church, one of the best known of the "wool churches".

treatment of woollen cloth. The splendid churches and half-timbered buildings of this area are the legacy of the great wealth obtained from the manufacture of cloth during the period of the "Old Draperies" (1300-1600).

By the time of the Norman invasion the villages along the Stour valley had become established in the locations they occupy today. Much of the forest had been cleared, yielding valuable agricultural and grazing land. Christianity was well established and the monks owned much of the land, on which they grazed large flocks of sheep. Although the wool was of poor quality, short and coarse, the region was in close proximity to the continent, where ready markets were found for it in Flanders, the Netherlands, the Rhine valley, Normandy, Germany and France.

During the fourteenth century, at the time of the Hundred Years War, many Flemish weavers emigrated to England when France threatened to annexe Flanders. Small groups of Flemish weavers settled in the villages along the Stour including Dedham, East Bergholt, Long Melford, Glemsford and Sudbury. The migration was encouraged by King Edward III, who had married a Flemish princess, Philippa of Hainault. The weavers brought with them fresh skills and techniques, which rejuvenated, if not founded, the cloth industry in the Stour valley.

Wool was spun using a distaff, a cleft stick about 3 feet long, which the seated spinner tucked under her left arm to hold the unspun wool. The thread was drawn out from the unspun wool and attached to a spindle which was then rotated under gravity with the spinner's right hand. The spinning wheel was not invented until 1530.

Writers differ with regard to the degree of twist given to the thread required for woollens, the cloth favoured in the Stour valley. While some state that it was strongly twisted to give it cohesion, others record that it was loosely spun and had little twist so that it would mat more readily during the fulling process. It is difficult to see how the individual spinners, women and children, throughout a town could produce a uniform thread using the primitive distaff. It seems more likely that the tighter, stronger threads would be selected for the warp, which runs the length of the cloth to give it strength, while the looser twisted wool was used for the weft, the thread carried across the warp by the shuttle. In this way the warp would impart strength to the cloth while the weft would be more easily matted over it. This was certainly the process used during the time of the "New Draperies" and is described in *The English Housewife* by Gervase Markham in 1611:

> "The better experienced make two manner of spinnings, and two sorts of thread, the one they call warp, the other weft; warp is spun close round and hard twisted, being strong and well smoothed, because it runs through the sleves, and also endureth the fretting and beating of the Beam; the weft is spun open, loose hollow and but half twisted, neither smoothed with the hand, nor made of any great strength, because it only crosseth the warp, without any violent straining and by reason of the softness thereof beddeth closer, and covereth the warp so well, that a very little beating in the mill bringeth it to a perfect cloth."

Undoubtedly the strength of the woollen cloth from the "Old Draperies" came from the fulling process rather than from the spinning. After weaving, the cloth was taken to the mill for fulling, which gave it the mat or felt appearance. The wet cloth was beaten with large hammers worked mechanically from the mill machinery, and then it was scrubbed with Fuller's earth (aluminium silicate) to cleanse the cloth and give it a good texture. The cloth was finally stretched out on wooden frames or tenters to dry it and to complete the bleaching process. The cloth was then dyed, usually a shade of blue using woad. Some wool was dyed before it was woven.

A fast flowing river was essential to provide power for the fulling process, and although none of the East Anglian rivers were ideal, the swifter flowing Stour favoured the production of woollen cloth in its valley. Woollens were manufactured at Cavendish, Clare, Dedham, East Bergholt, Glemsford and Sudbury.

The clothiers, originally wool brokers who traded in both the wool and the finished products, eventually controlled all aspects of the industry from the spinning to dyeing and finishing. They controlled a great but largely self-employed work force and became very rich, the most notable being the Spring family at Lavenham. It was their wealth which financed the magnificent wool churches seen throughout the valley, and the clothiers became the elite of Tudor society.

A demonstration of spinning at Southfields, Dedham. The spinning wheel did not come into use until late in the history of the cloth trade in Suffolk.

The reasons for the decline of the cloth industry towards the end of the sixteenth century and at the beginning of the next are complex. This period of the "Old Draperies" had witnessed the climax of medieval culture, the destruction of half the population of England by the Black Death and the disruption of the economic organisation of England by the Wars of the Roses. Besides this, lack of organisation by the Suffolk clothiers and the close proximity of Suffolk to London led to a takeover by the London merchants, sometimes giving the Suffolk people less than a fair deal. Religious wars on the Continent affected the customers of the East Anglian trade and there was a growing demand for the lighter fabrics being produced in Europe, particularly in the warmer countries which were now being opened up by Spanish and Portuguese exploration. A combination of these events brought about the downfall of the woollen cloth industry.

The introduction of methods of manufacturing the new cloth by the Dutch and Huguenot immigrants, escaping from religious persecution in their homelands at the beginning of the seventeenth century, only delayed the final collapse until the end of that century. Even an Act of Parliament passed in 1678, which ensured that the dead were buried in woollen shrouds, did little to revive the industry.

The Dutch were not as popular as the Fleming immigrants had been and so they tended to congregate in isolated communities in the larger towns. As a result Norwich and Colchester became the main centres for the "New Draperies", and to a lesser extent Sudbury and Long Melford. The women and children in the smaller Stour villages eked out an impoverished existence by using the newly invented spinning wheels to spin yarn for the Norwich weavers.

The decline of the "New Draperies", never very evident in the Stour valley, was brought about by the introduction of new fibres from abroad, particularly cotton, silk and Indian calico. Gradually the cloth industry moved north to Yorkshire and Lancashire, where the weavers were quick to take advantage of new inventions, such as the spinning jenny and the flying shuttle, and of the fast-flowing rivers from the Pennines which together with coal were able to produce the power for the new machinery.

The Stour was one of the first English rivers to be made navigable to barge traffic. After the Civil War the population of England, and particularly London, increased rapidly, creating an increasing demand for food. East Anglia, at the forefront of the agricultural revolution, possessed the rich fertile soil on which to grow it and the rivers provided the means of transporting it to the growing Metropolis.

As early as 1628 Charles I had made grants of letters patent to Arnold Spencer to make the River Stour navigable, but it was not until 1705, in the reign of Queen Anne, that a Navigation Act was passed which permitted work to begin. It is not certain when the first barge reached Sudbury, but it seems this would be by 1714 as a map of that date shows the warehouses in position at Sudbury. Thirteen locks had to be constructed along the twenty-five miles of river and the course of the Stour was changed in some places. A hundred Commissioners of the Navigation were appointed to act as referees in case of dispute between the users and the administrators of the Navigation, and when all but two of these had died by 1780 a second Navigation Act appointed new commissioners, which included Golding Constable, the artist's father, and Gainsborough's brothers, Samuel and John. The Commissioners met annually at the *Queen's Head* at Nayland.

The barges operated in pairs, one towed astern of the other by a horse. As it had proved impossible to acquire the right of access for a continuous towpath on one side of the river, the Navigation Company being one of the few who did not purchase the land for the towpath but instead paid tolls to the landowners, the horse was required not only to jump every stile along the way

Flatford lock, now restored to working order, and, opposite, an old horse-drawn Stour lighter being rebuilt by the River Stour Trust.

but also to cross the river no fewer than thirty-three times. As there were only sixteen bridges, the horses were trained to cross by stepping or leaping on to the barge, straw being put down to soften the landing, and then jumping off on to the opposite bank, a method of crossing the river unique to the Stour.

The barges were constructed of timber and built locally along the river. Constable's picture, *Boat Building at Flatford*, shows a barge under construction there. Each barge was approximately 45 feet long with a maximum width of about 10 feet and had a draught of nearly 3 feet when fully laden with 13 tons of cargo. The dimensions of the barge are often quoted erroneously elsewhere: the length of 27 feet is incorrect and the cargo of 26 tons capacity refers to the load carried by a pair of barges. The width of the barge is sometimes quoted as 10 feet 9 inches while the locks are 10 feet wide—a case of having to hold your breath and barge your way through!

With increasing competition from the railway, opened to Sudbury in 1849, an attempt was made about 1860 to power the barges with steam engines to replace the horses. This might have been successful if purpose-built steam barges had been constructed instead of putting the engines into the existing barges. The draught of these was so small that the propeller at times stuck out above the water level. The project was abandoned about 1880 and the barges sold, although members of the River Stour Trust have recently salvaged a propeller, part of its shaft and a section of steam boiler from the river entrance to the Sudbury basin. However, a steam-powered dredger introduced to the river in 1879 proved very successful in keeping the river clear from obstruction and greatly facilitated the navigation.

The river traffic was at its busiest during the lifetime of John Constable (1776-1837) whose paintings, including *The Leaping Horse, White Horse* and *Flatford Mill*, not only portray the beauty of the Stour valley but also provide an accurate historical record of the wealth of human activity which went on along the river.

At the beginning of the first world war many of the old barges were sunk in the river outside Sudbury at Ballingdon Cut, to prevent the Germans using them if they ever invaded, or so it is said. The River Stour Trust has recently recovered and restored one of these barges as well as renovating the old navigation basin at Sudbury where the barges once tied up. The restored barge will be kept in the navigation basin alongside the old granary, now converted into a theatre.

The short two-mile tidal crossing from Brantham mill to Mistley provided the most difficult part of the journey for the bargemen. The horses were left at Brantham and the journey was completed with the help of wind or tide. If this failed the barges were pushed along with a pole or quant.

If the wind was favourable the skipper would hoist a make-shift square sail made from old sacking to assist his passage across this dangerous stretch of water. At Mistley quay the cargo was transferred into the Thames sailing or spritsail barges for the sea journey to London.

Unlike the river barges, which are now extinct, a few spritsail barges still earn their keep as holiday craft or providing school children with educational cruises round the coast, while others such as the *May* are used for conferences and are entered for the annual barge races. There is no finer sight than to see these barges coming up the Stour on a full tide with red-ochre sails glistening in the sunlight and contrasted sharply against the green wooded banks of the river and the blue sky and sea.

The spritsail barge developed from the fourteenth-century Thames lighter which transferred cargo from the shore to sailing ships anchored mid-stream in the Thames. Gradually the barges were made seaworthy; cargo holds were fitted with hatches, the hull modified and sails added to make them suitable for coastal voyages. Their flat bottoms and shallow draught, it was the idle boast of a skipper that he could sail his barge across land on a heavy dew,

Sailing barges at Mistley quay, from where grain and malt was shipped to London.

The *Kimberley*, a Thames spritsail barge, on the Stour during one of the annual barge races.

made them particularly suitable for work on the east coast rivers, where they could go over the sand-bars and mud flats at low tide. The barges have no keel but lee-boards are fitted on either side and can be lowered to prevent the barges drifting sideways. The spritsail from which the barge takes its name is the mainsail which is supported by a diagonal spar—the sprit. This simple design, which was first used by the Dutch during the fourteenth century on their fighting ships, enables the mainsail and mast to be raised or lowered very easily to allow passage under bridges and allowed the barge to be handled if necessary by only two people.

Thames barges were built along the Stour at Harwich, Mistley and Brantham. Richard Rigby opened a shipyard at Mistley in 1753 from which came men-of-war including in 1798 the *Amphion*, which for a time was Nelson's flagship, besides the barges built by the Horlock family, the Mistley bargebuilders and owners.

From the time Mistley quay was opened in 1730 until the end of the first world war Mistley was a thriving port importing coal from Sunderland and Newcastle for the gas works at Sudbury, foreign grain for the maltings and timber from Scandinavia. Grain, bricks, chalk and flour, with hay for the London cab horses, went to the capital and malt was exported to the Guinness brewery at Dublin. The barges sailed between Mistley and Butterman's Bay near Pin Mill on the Orwell to unload the grain ships which anchored there. Three small spritsail barges, the *Cygnet* (25 tons), the *Muriel* (23 tons) and the *Alice* (30 tons) operated within the Stour estuary, calling at farms along the river to collect wheat, straw and barley to be taken to Mistley for delivery to London.

Jetties were built for the barges at Holbrook, Harkstead and Erwarton, from where farmer Wrinch's stack barges, (stackies—barges loaded with hay on their deck) sailed. If a jetty was uneconomical a hard (roadway out into the river) was constructed upon which the barges could sit at low tide while the wagons or tumbrils off-loaded their goods into the barge.

The barges could not compete with the railways after their introduction during the middle of the nineteenth century. The line to Manningtree from Colchester was completed in 1846 and to Sudbury in 1849. For a time improvements to the navigation of the river allowed the barges to compete economically with the railway, but by the end of the first world war the river trade was almost at an end. The last barge reached Sudbury in 1914, although at least one barge continued to work between Brantham and Dedham mill until 1931.

Now the railway has succumbed to road transport. The railway track upstream from Sudbury has been removed, leaving a delightful country walk as far as Rodbridge corner. One wonders, now that the price of petrol has soared astronomically and the world shortage of oil becomes more acute, how long it will be before the barges return to the Stour. Already Britain's entry to the Common Market has given new impetus to the port of Mistley, from which a regular cargo service has been introduced to Rotterdam. More shippers are turning to motor-driven barges as an effective and economical method of handling goods between ports, the continent and London. The railway now supports rather than competes with the river traffic plying the estuary, and once again the tidal river is proving its value in transporting cargo economically as it has done in previous centuries.

CHAPTER TWO

At the Beginning—The Source to Stoke-by-Clare

THE STOUR rises on the border of Cambridgeshire with Suffolk near Weston Green on Wratting Common. It is a natural border formed where the London clay to the east, which once supported dense forest, meets the chalk uplands, a continuation of the Chiltern Hills.

Along this track, the Icknield Way, primitive people passed on their way between Avebury and Thetford in the Norfolk Brecklands. This chalk ridge has been a major route across England throughout history, and the A11 now follows it for some distance. This area was border country between the kingdoms of Mercia and East Anglia and marked the limit reached by the Saxons, who followed the Stour valley upstream from the sea to penetrate the forest, which they cleared so as to make their homes in it. The village name of Weston at the start of the Stour is derived from the Saxon, meaning western homestead.

Murder was commonplace during medieval times and a Norman soldier out alone was considered fair game by the native Saxons. A five-pound fine (equivalent to about £300 now) was imposed as a deterrent on any parish in which a murdered body was found. To avoid paying the fine, the murderers would dump the body over the border in a neighbouring parish. One unfortunate who was murdered in the parish of Stetchworth, south of Newmarket, in 1295 was passed from one parish to the next until he was finally buried on Weston Green.

A small cluster of farm outbuildings standing on an exposed and windy plateau where the Stour runs off Wratting Common is known as Moyne's Farm. It is named after the hall which stood at this lonely place at the time of Domesday. Moyne's Hall was the home of the beautiful Eddeva Pulchra, Edith the Fair, said by some to have been the widow of Edward the Confessor, while others believe her to have been Edith Swansneck, King Harold's favourite mistress.

Several small streams drain Wratting Common, some of them joining to form the Stour near to the Three Horseshoes, a delightful thatched sixteenth-century farmhouse at Weston Green. Until 1957 it was a public house, visited on one occasion by the Duke of York, later to become George VI, and the Duke of Kent when they picnicked in the field opposite the pub.

The river meanders westwards for a couple of miles to Carlton through undulating countryside, now denuded of most of its trees to expose rich agricultural land. This is one of very few places in England where the very rare Oxlip plants are found growing, in the remaining copses of Weston Woods.

The Stour emerges from Sipsey bridge on the B1061 to turn south from Cambridgeshire into Suffolk. Seven churches along the river bank mark its course for the next five miles. Each one undoubtedly stands on a site cleared by the Saxon settlers, their wooden churches being replaced by Norman stone buildings, parts of which remain in several of the present churches.

Great Bradley church, the first the river meets on its way downstream, has the best Tudor brick porch in Suffolk, built, it is believed, by Henry VIII's own brickmaker. An unique fireplace on which Holy wafers were cooked is built into the base of the tower, and the church door behind the south porch was modelled by the Normans on a design introduced into England by the Romans.

Little Bradley church has a nave and chancel which are Anglo-Saxon. It contains many brasses, one of which commemorates John Daye (died 1584), the prominent sixteenth-century printer, who printed works by Latimer, Archbishop Parker and Foxe's *The Book of Martyrs*. This propagandist history

The author near the source of the river at Weston Green, in Cambridgeshire.

of the English church which described the persecution of the English protestants during the reign of Mary was often placed beside the Bible in the parish church. Daye was the first person to be admitted to the livery of the Company of Stationers, which received its charter from Queen Mary, and became Master of the Company in 1580. His name was perpetuated by his twenty-six children from his two marriages and in the John Day Publishing Company of New York.

A Norman font dates Little Thurlow church, while Great Thurlow church stands between the river and the Georgian Hall in the most picturesque and best-kept village in this area.

Great Wratting church was restored by the Rt. Hon. W. H. Smith, founder of the newsagents of that name, who had taken possession of Great Wratting manor in 1885. This manor was part of the dowry of Anne of Cleves when she married Henry VIII in 1540. Little Wratting church is beautiful in its simplicity, its Anglo-Saxon nave surmounted by an oak-framed bell turret with a short shingled spire. It overlooks the stark undulating Suffolk countryside and also, unfortunately, a modern meat factory which processes pigs into pork pies.

Across the main Haverhill to Bury road (A143) stands Kedington church on a hill at the foot of which the Stour flows under a nineteenth-century mill, now used as an artists' studio and residence. Next door is a delightful thatched cottage which once formed part of a dairy farm. Mrs Skilton, in her eighties, who ran the farm with her husband, remembers delivering the milk in pails suspended from a yoke across her shoulders.

The church has been called the Westminster Abbey of Suffolk because of its many tombstones and memorials to the Barnardiston family. The atmosphere inside is mysterious and uncertain, making the visitor apprehensive. It is as if the spirits who have gone before are wary lest the intruder interrupts their requiem.

A Saxon church, parts of which are contained in the present vaults, was built here on the remains of a Roman villa, which still exist.

From Kedington the Stour continues south to Wixoe, meandering through a wide valley flanked by low hills. During the seventeenth century the river, known as the Burne, flowed into a lake then considered to be the source of the Stour. Robert Reyce described the lake in the *Suffolk Breviary* of 1618 as "This lake of 20 acres in compasse at the least, is the head and source of that great river Stoure, which divideth Suffolk from Essex. From this poole or lake it takes its course Eastwards through Clare, Long Melford and Sudbury until it comes to the Flemmish sea." Another tributary which still flows off Wratting Common and through Haverhill also joined the lake known as Stoure Meare, from which came the name of the village of Sturmer.

Haverhill, now a thriving modern industrial town, was one of the first to participate in the town expansion schemes of the 1950's to accommodate overspill population from London. The town, however, is of ancient foundation, having been sited originally on the old Roman road from Colchester to Cambridge. At one time it boasted ancient earthworks and a castle which dated back to Roman or Anglo-Saxon times, but all of it now seems to have become submerged beneath large housing estates. During the Norman period the small settlement belonged to one Haver, who gave his name to the town (Haver was also the name given to a male goat and a word for oats) when it formed part of the Honor of Clare and came under the control of the Earls of Clare, who resided in the neighbouring castle.

In common with the other Stour towns, Haverhill was a centre for the medieval wool trade, making Linsey-Woolsey; a coarse homespun woollen and linen cloth. Unfortunately because of a fire which ravaged the town in 1667 there is only one remaining example of the half-timbered framed buildings which are so characteristic of the Stour towns. This is the old vicarage which Henry VIII gave to Anne of Cleves as a present on their wedding day in 1540. Now known as Cleve House, it is used as an office block for a large industrial company.

The three-decker pulpit in Kedington church, with the hour glass which was used for timing the sermon in days when brevity was not a valued attribute on the preacher's part.

The firm of Daniel Gurteen perpetuates the traditional textile industry, which gradually replaced the woollen industry. Today the firm, which has its headquarters in the High Street, manufactures lightweight jackets and trousers, while another department produces deck-chair and awning fabrics made from nylon and polyester yarn. Matmaking, another industry which took the place of weaving woollens when this industry declined, is also perpetuated by Gurteens.

At the time of the Napoleonic wars (1785-1815) copper currency became scarce and as a result local tradesmen issued substitute tokens. One at Haverhill, the Fincham Halfpenny, was issued by the Haverhill Manufactory and could be redeemed at John Fincham's retail store. The token was inscribed on one side with the figure of a man weaving, and on the reverse was the figure of a hind's head, which has become the trade mark for the firm of Daniel Gurteen.

In 1780 William Addis made a toothbrush from horsehair and bone for his own personal use, but he soon found a ready market for his invention through the London booksellers, who at that time were the main retailers of patent medicines and chemists' sundries. The firm of William Addis eventually became the first manufacturer of toothbrushes in the world. In 1945 they acquired the premises and grounds belonging to the old silk mill at Haverhill on which to build a new factory, and now 41 million toothbrushes a year are made at Haverhill, each one being individually inspected before leaving the factory.

On the bend of the Stour at Wixoe a modern water pumping station abstracts water from the river and transfers 24 million gallons a day to the river Pant which rises between Wimbish and Saffron Walden. The Pant becomes the River Blackwater at Braintree and feeds the Essex reservoirs at Abberton and Hanningfield. It is all part of the Great Ouse-Essex scheme which takes surplus water from the Great Ouse river system at Denver in Norfolk for use in the densely populated areas of Essex a hundred miles away. The water is channelled from Denver to Blackdyke fifteen miles to the south-east, from where it is drawn off into a tunnel which terminates at Kennett. Pumps lift the water from the tunnel and through a nine-mile-long pipeline over the watershed and into the river Stour at Kirtling Green.

Part of this discharge is drawn off at Wixoe, eight miles downstream, and pumped the six miles over further watersheds to the river Pant at Great Sampford. The balance of water in the River Stour passes downstream, eventually to be abstracted at Langham and Stratford St Mary for the reservoirs at Abberton and Hanningfield. These waterworks form a vital link in the water distribution "ring main" envisaged to rectify the main deficiency of water supply in South East England.*

*Taken from *The Ely Ouse-Essex Scheme,* Essex River Authority.

◀ Kedington mill, now the residence of an artist.

From Wixoe the Stour flows eastwards through some of the prettiest and most historic villages in England. It is difficult to realise, looking across the wide expanse of their village greens edged with picturesque thatched cottages, that this was once one of the most populous regions of England.

Stoke-by-Clare is the first of the villages through which the Stour flows on its easterly course. Unspoilt by tourists or commercial enterprises and standing beside the river amidst acres of tree-studded parkland, it is the most restful of the Stour villages.

Stoke College, an independent boarding school for boys and girls, stands on the site of a Benedictine Priory, which was established in 1124 for the monks of Bec. The monastery at Bec in Normandy was one of the main centres of medieval christianity. Parts of the old priory are incorporated in the present buildings, which were erected during the seventeenth and eighteenth centuries.

In 1415 the priory became a college for secular priests and remained so until its dissolution by Edward VI in 1548, when it was granted to Sir John Cheke, who was required to surrender it to the Exchequer on Mary's accession to the throne in 1553. The priory had survived the dissolution of the monasteries ordered by Henry VIII probably because Matthew Parker was both dean of the college and chaplain to the king.

Cardinal Wolsey made an abortive attempt to close the college in 1526 and to appropriate its funds towards two large collegiate colleges he was building at Ipswich and Oxford. Unfortunately for Wolsey, the college was under the patronage of the Queens of England. Katharine of Aragon foiled the Cardinal by taking possession of the title deeds to the college.

Matthew Parker was the last dean of Stoke College. He was born in Norwich in 1504, graduated from Corpus Christi College, Cambridge, and after being ordained became Master of his college and then Vice-Chancellor of the University and ultimately Archbishop of Canterbury. In 1535 Parker became chaplain to Anne Boleyn and she then appointed him dean of her college at Stoke. Elizabeth of York, wife of Henry VII, first inherited the estate at Stoke, which then became the property of the Queens of England until its secularisation. Her portrait is immortalised on the deck of playing cards which were invented at this time.

After attending his queen, Anne Boleyn, at her execution in 1536, Parker was appointed chaplain to the King, a post he held while remaining dean at Stoke. During this period Parker met Margaret Harlestone; he wished to marry her but could not do so because of the Roman law of celibacy for priests. This ban on marriage was lifted by Edward VI in 1547 and the couple then married and took up residence at Corpus Christi, Cambridge. When Mary came to the throne all clergy were required to renounce their marriages or lose their livings. Parker chose the latter.

Stoke College, which stands on the site of a Benedictine Priory.

On the accession of Queen Elizabeth Parker was appointed Archbishop of Canterbury. At this time the Church of England maintained its position as a true part of the Catholic church, while claiming the right to self-government. The Archbishop was able to walk the tight rope between the extremes of both religious houses. He died in 1575 and was buried in Lambeth Palace.

During his time as dean of Stoke College, Parker founded the first grammar school in the town for the education of the sons of rich and poor alike. Parents who could not afford the fees were asked to work at the school. Villagers told me that the school building is probably one of the buildings standing to the left of the entrance to the present college, but this is not certain.

The present independent school which occupies the site of Stoke College was founded at Clare after the second world war with the name of Grenville College and moved to the present larger premises in 1957. The name of the college was changed to Stoke College in 1973 to associate it with the ancient place of learning.

Before leaving Stoke College mention must be made of the two misers, Sir Hervey Elwes, the last baronet, and his nephew John Meggot who, on inheriting the college, now a house, from his uncle in 1763, was ordered to assume the name and arms of Elwes. It is reputed that John's mother was so mean that she died of starvation, while it was believed that John was the richest commoner in England, having inherited a quarter of a million pounds from his uncle.

This was no reason, however, for not enforcing the most rigorous economies in running his household. Windows were repaired with brown paper. He saved fuel in winter by either sitting in the greenhouse or with his servant, and he collected straw and crows' nests for a fire. He had only one servant who looked after the stables, the cattle, the horses, a pack of hounds, his only luxury, and performed the myriad duties associated with a large estate. His master referred to him as "an idle dog who wanted to be paid for nothing". When travelling on horseback he avoided all turnpikes and public houses, sustaining himself with only hard-boiled eggs and crusts. He died unmarried in 1789, bequeathing half a million pounds to his two sons.

The village church of St John the Baptist stands at the entrance to Stoke College opposite an early-sixteenth-century dovecote with an unusual grille pattern resembling a portcullis made from blue header bricks. Inside the church is one of the smallest pulpits in the county, having a diameter of only twenty-eight inches. A stained glass window dated about 1480 contains a picture of a French smock windmill and is a reminder of the close association of this area with France. It is probably the earliest picture of this type of windmill in England. A wall painting of the Doom or Last Judgement was discovered in 1947 behind the church organ. It shows Christ sitting on a rainbow judging the living and the dead, while beneath him the Virgin Mary leads a procession of the saved and Gluttony, holding a large flagon, is seen walking to hell. The painting is believed to be one of the last such religious wall paintings to be done in England, probably between 1553 and 1558 during the Roman Catholic revival in Queen Mary's reign.

From this idyllic corner of Suffolk it is just two miles along the river to Clare, the most ancient country town on the Stour.

Clare is approached from Stoke along the Nethergate, a wide spacious tree-lined street flanked by beautiful old houses whose picturesque gardens reach down to the river. This street takes its name from the lower gate which defended the castle entrance. Along this street would have come kings and princes with their colourful attendant processions on their way to the Norman castle.

The stature and prominence of Clare in medieval times, together with a sense of history, radiates from every building, adding to the old world charm of this town. Many of its half-timbered ancient buildings, some say too many, are occupied by antique shops, each selling its own brand of historical relics.

During the thirteenth century the Clare family barons were among the most powerful in the country. At least thirteen of them were at the signing of the Magna Carta and they had estates in twenty English counties.

William the Conqueror gave the town, along with a number of other manors in the locality, collectively known as the Honor of Clare, to his kinsman Richard Fitz Gilbert, a bastard son of Richard Duke of Normandy. His descendants took the name of Clare, which may have derived from an old British name meaning "clear", a reference to the brightness of the water of the River Stour. It was Richard's son Gilbert who gave the castle church at Clare to the Benedictine monks, and in turn Gilbert's son Richard transferred them to the priory at Stoke when he took up residence in the castle. His brother Walter founded Tintern Abbey, while Gilbert was given Cardigan by Henry I.

The Clare family gained the title Earl of Gloucester when this Richard's grandson married Amicia, the daughter of William, Earl of Gloucester. Their

A French smock windmill portrayed in a window of Stoke-by-Clare church.

grandson founded the House of Austin Friars in the town in 1248, and his son Gilbert married Joan of Acre, the daughter of King Edward I, to begin the connection between the Clare family and the monarchy of England. Acre is a town in Palestine, now Israel, where Joan was born. The royal couple had four children. Their son Gilbert was killed at the battle of Bannockburn in 1314 and their daughter Elizabeth, whose first of three marriages was to John de Burgh, founded Clare College, the second oldest of the Cambridge colleges. It was first founded as University Hall by its chancellor, Richard de Badew, in 1326 but it soon ran into financial difficulties and was then rescued by Lady Clare, Elizabeth de Burgh, and renamed Clare Hall in 1338. It became known as Clare College in 1856.

Lady Clare's granddaughter, also Elizabeth de Burgh, married Prince Lionel, Earl of Ulster and third son of King Edward III. The Earl took the title Duke of Clarence, further perpetuating the name of Clare.

The carved base of an oriel window believed to have come from Clare castle but now incorporated into the *Swan Inn*.

The castle was once a royal residence. It is known that both Edward I, Edward II and Henry III stayed here. Today there is nothing left of the castle apart from one wall of the keep, which overlooks the town from the summit of its man-made mound, and parts of the ramparts and walls which once surrounded the inner and outer castle baileys. Unfortunately these were badly damaged when the railway was brought to Clare and the station built within the castle precincts.

The railway was closed under the Beeching axe and the grounds have been converted into a delightful country park, through which one can stroll or picnic among the willows beside the Stour. In 1865 a gold cross and chain, which it is thought belonged to Edward III, was discovered within the castle grounds. A cavity in the cross contained a small fragment of wood and a granite pebble. The wood was allegedly a fragment of the true Cross while the pebble may have been a memorial from a sacred locality in the Holy land. The cross is now kept at Windsor Castle.

Above the doorway of the *Swan Inn* is an elaborately carved base of an oriel window, which dates from 1415 and is believed to have come from the castle. The central figure of a chained swan may have been part of the Arms of the Welsh Bohun family which Henry IV adopted when he married Mary Bohun. The swan is flanked on the left by the Arms of Mortimer and de Burgh and on the right by the Arms of England and France.

The castle fell into ruins during the seventeenth century, crumbled by wind and weather; there is no recorded battle at Clare. Robert Reyce wrote of the castle in 1618, "Time, the consumer of all things, hath left nothing but ruins on a beautiful situation."

Just across the river from the castle stands Clare Priory, which housed the first Order of Augustinian or Austin Friars to be founded in England in 1248 A.D. They should not be confused with the Benedictine monks who had come to Clare castle earlier before being transferred to Stoke.

The friars, unlike monks, were not confined to their religious houses but were free to move about the countryside begging, preaching and teaching.

St Augustine was born in Tagaste, North Africa, in 354 A.D. and brought up by his mother, later St Monica, in the Christian faith, which as a young man he rejected. Later he relented, was ordained and became the Bishop of Hippo. The order follows the rules referred to St Augustine but its origin is in dispute. Certainly Austin Canons were founded in Avignon in 1061 and first appeared in Britain about 1100.

The most progressive of these were the Friars of Tuscany who spread into France, from where they were invited to Clare. Here the Friars remained until 1538 when the priory was closed by order of Henry VIII and the friars were pensioned off. The priory became Crown property and then passed into private ownership until 1953 when the Friars, through the generosity of the last private owners, were again able to occupy their priory.

The Prior's house, built in the fourteenth century and re-modelled during the fifteenth, is well preserved, having been in private ownership for many years. Only one wall, however, remains of the great monastic church in which was buried Joan of Acre, daughter of Edward I, and Lionel, Duke of Clarence, the third son of Edward III, whose body was brought from Pavia in Italy to be buried alongisde his wife Elizabeth de Burgh.

Clare Priory, now again occupied by Augustinian Friars after having been a private house for several centuries.

Growing vines and making wine was an important occupation in the Stour valley during the Middle Ages. Every manor and monastery had its own vineyard and Clare was no exception, having at one time twenty-two acres of vines. It was once thought that Clare gave its name to Claret; the English name given to the collection of light red wines from the Bordeaux and Gascony regions of France. The connection between England and this part of France, both of which formed part of the Angevin Empire under Henry II, resulted in the importation of these cheap wines, which could be bought for one penny a gallon in the fourteenth century. An eighteenth century wine merchant's list stated; "The name Claret is derived from Clare Priory on the borders of Suffolk, originally in Essex, the river Stour having altered its course. The Lord of the Manor of Clare had vineyards in Bordeaux, France, and the wine shipped to this place (for Clare was then open to navigation for sea-going ships by means of the Stour) was known as the wine of Clare and nicknamed Clarette."

However, it is known that the French referred to these wines as *CLAIRET* even before they were imported into England. The Romans, who, it is believed, introduced the vine into England, referred to wine as *VINUM CLARATUM*, wine which has been clarified, and *VINUM CLARUM*, wine of a naturally clear nature, and it is probably from these terms that the word Claret is derived. Today in the next village of Cavendish the vine has been re-introduced, and the English wine industry is being re-established in the Stour valley.

In Pepys' mind "no wine out of France was more mellow."

The Priest's House at Clare seen from the church.

CHAPTER THREE

Cavendish to Glemsford and the River Glem

THE perfect English village scene, a gently sloping village green with its church, public house and thatched cottages picturesquely grouped together, greets the motorist as he turns the corner of Stour Street to enter Cavendish. Pictures of Cavendish typify the English scene and appear regularly in books and magazines.

Sir Alfred Munnings wrote of this scene, "I know of no better grouping than those thatched lime-washed cottages at the top end of the Green clustered round the church. An incomparable English scene! Alas! no cattle or sheep are about the Green as of yore."

Behind the church stands Nether Hall, a fifteenth-century building which was once the original village manor. It is now the home of farmer Basil Ambrose, who cultivates the two hundred acres of land his family have held for three hundred years. He has the distinction not only of planting one of the first vineyards in the Stour valley since the Middle Ages but of having his wine judged to be one of the best two in England at the English wine competition held at Christie's in 1975. Since then Cavendish Manor wine has graced the table for a dinner held for the Commonwealth Heads of Government, and British Airways chose it to serve with their in-flight meals on St George's Day, 1978.

The vagaries of the weather are the vigneron's greatest headache. Although vines can grow almost anywhere, ideally they require a long hot summer to ripen the grapes and a sufficiently long cool, dry winter in which the vines can rest and withdraw the sap from their canes. This restricts the best growing areas in the Northern Hemisphere to between 30 and 50 degrees of latitude. Although East Anglia is just outside these limits, the introduction of hardier strains of vines has made English wine production a viable proposition.

Basil Ambrose planted ten acres of his land with Müller Thurgau vines, a Riesling-Sylvaner cross that in Germany now rivals their most important Riesling. Cavendish wine is a dry white wine with a delicate flowery smell and entrancing taste. It has been described by its Continental rivals with the usual wine jargon as "a wine with an attractive bouquet which followed through in the taste"; "a fine elegant and nicely balanced wine"; "a wine with a splendid personality and intriguing bouquet and a very distinguished character."

A ton of grapes produces on average a thousand bottles of wine, and a vineyard must produce at least two to three tons of grapes to an acre for it to be profitable. The years 1974 to 1976 were good ones for Cavendish wine. Production leapt from 1,500 bottles in 1974 to 30,000 bottles in 1976. A fine dry autumn saved the 1977 crop after a wet summer, but the following year was very wet and yielded only a twentieth of the previous year's crop.

Cavendish is one of seven hundred members of the English Vineyards Association, whose total products are valued at a million pounds on the retail market. About five million pounds of land and assets are tied up in the industry, which produces about 500,000 bottles of wine a year. A system of Appellation Controlée, similar to that in operation by the E.E.C. on the Continent, was set up in 1979 by the E.V.A. who have just judged eight English wines, including Cavendish Manor, to qualify for their seal of approval, the guarantee of a top quality wine.

Vendange takes place during October; that is, if the weather has been kind, the grapes have escaped the mildew Botrytis Cinerea, which can give the wine a nasty taste, and the thrushes and blackbirds have not consumed the crop. A dawn to dusk bird-scaring patrol is mounted a month before the grapes are gathered. After the grapes are pressed, the juice is filtered and fermented in large vats. Six months later, the winefest, the first Cavendish wine of the season is ready for our delight.

The five famous fifteenth-century almshouses stand beside the green at Hyde Park Corner, a most inappropriate name for such a tranquil scene. In 1958 these cottages were in such a bad state of repair that villagers under the chairmanship of Tom Ambrose, and with the assistance of Sir Alfred Munnings, purchased and restored the cottages. Unfortunately they were burnt in 1972 and the villagers again had to find sufficient money to add to the insurance payment to reach a figure of £22,000 required to rebuild the cottages. It was money well spent. The cottages stand as a testimony to the skill of the local craftsmen who restored the buildings, which won the 1973 West Suffolk architectural award.

The cottages are administered by the George Savage Charity, set up in 1938. George was a local boy who spent several winters on local farms before making his fortune with a London cafe business. When he died in the 1930s he left £14,000 for the sick and poor of his native village.

"Unions strike for higher wages", "Government enforces wage freeze" are news headlines as familiar today as they were applicable to industrial relations as far back as the fourteenth century. After the Black Death had swept the country for the first time in 1348, reducing the population by almost half, the labouring class who had previously been tied to their master's land gradually became free men and with the shortage of labour they were able to demand higher wages. The Government tried to keep down wages and prices by law, a

Gathering the grapes from Basil Ambrose's vineyard at Cavendish. These grapes provide one of the very best of English wines.

familiar phrase and fruitless task, with the Statute of Labourers in 1350 which laid down that the rates of pay were not to be more than those appertaining in 1347. An attempt was also made to restrict the mobility of workmen in search of higher remuneration.

When in 1380 the Chancellor of England, Simon of Sudbury, imposed the third poll tax on the people of England to finance the French war, the labourers struck, rebelled and rioted. John Wrawe, a former priest from Beccles, led riots in the Stour valley starting at Liston, near Long Melford, and then marched with his mob on Cavendish. Here the rebels broke into the church tower and took away valuables belonging to Sir John Cavendish, formerly the King's Chief Justice. The judiciary had made themselves very unpopular by trying to enforce the Law of Statute.

From Cavendish they marched down the valley to Long Melford, wrecking Pentlow Hall on the way, and then went to Bury St Edmunds. Meanwhile, some of the insurgents doubled back to Cavendish to capture Sir John. According to one account he was dragged from his mansion (I was told it is the house on the main road on the opposite side of the green nearest to Clare) and taken to Bury St Edmunds where he was beheaded. An alternative version (*The Peasants Revolt*, by Ronald Webber) states that he escaped the mob but was recaptured and beheaded as he attempted to cross the river by the ferry at Brandon. His head was then taken to Bury St Edmunds.

In London the final confrontation between the rebels, led by Wat Tyler, and the King took place at Smithfield. In the course of an affray, Tyler was struck down by the Lord Mayor of London, Sir William Walworth, and killed by one of the king's esquires. He was named as John Standwick, while another story refers to him as the son of Sir John Cavendish.

A sixteenth-century farmhouse, pink painted, plastered and timber framed, stands in beautiful grounds near the Stour. Since the mid 50's it has been the headquarters of the Sue Ryder Foundation; a home for the handicapped of different age groups and Lady Ryder's base, where she works and also lives with her husband, Group Captain Leonard Cheshire, V.C.

Sue Ryder was born in Leeds and grew up in the full awareness of the appalling poverty that existed in the town's slums. She visited people living in those dreadful conditions, and as a child was introduced to suffering humanity, both in the big cities and in the rural areas. Part of her childhood was spent in the lovely village of Thurlow in the Stour Valley. At the beginning of the second world war she worked in a local hospital looking after evacuees and the wounded from France before joining the First Aid Nursing Yeomanry (F.A.N.Y.).

She was posted to the Special Operations Executive (S.O.E.), those exceptionally brave "Bods" (the term is now affectionately used for patients in the Sue Ryder Homes) who as special agents carried on the war behind enemy lines. It was while listening to the "Bods" talking before going on their missions that the idea for the Sue Ryder Foundation germinated. She recalls in her autobiography, *And the Morrow is Theirs,* "I began to think of ways in which the qualities they possessed and showed—tolerance, faith, courage, humour and gaiety—might be perpetuated. I thought that instead of trying to remember all those who had died fighting or in camps by means of a plaque or monument, one should go out and provide assistance and comfort to those who are sick, and in need, wherever they might be, regardless of nationality or religion, creating in this a 'living memorial' to the dead."

Sue Ryder's work took her into the ruins of post-war Europe to help those of all age groups who had endured indescribable suffering.

Sue remarked "even after so many years, many of us find it quite impossible to describe what we saw. I find my own voice breaks as the memories come back to my mind."

After the war Sue Ryder continued with relief work with several organisations before striking out on her own. Her work at this time consisted of hospital visiting, the provision of medical aid, a holiday scheme for the disabled, and prison visiting. In the immediate aftermath of war some people in Europe took personal retribution against the Germans, and those found guilty of murder were either shot or imprisoned under martial law by the allies. It was these prisoners in whom Sue Ryder took a personal interest. She founded her first home at Bad Nauheim in Germany for discharged prisoners.

Sue Ryder's father died in 1942 and after the war her mother moved to the village of Cavendish. Then in 1953-54 Sue Ryder acquired her property by the river and set up the headquarters of her Foundation here, as well as converting the house into a home for the disabled.

One of the "bods" at the Sue Ryder Home at Cavendish enjoys a quiet moment with the ducks which come up from the Stour.

The aim of the Foundation is "To render personal service to those in need and to give affection to those who are unloved, regardless of age, race or creed, as part of the Family of Man." Their emblem is a sprig of rosemary for remembrance "There's rosemary, that's for remembrance; pray, love, remember: and there is pansies, that's for thoughts" (Shakespeare—*Hamlet.*)

The Home at Cavendish is informal, friendly, cheerful and homely. It has been considerably extended since its early days and further extensions, including the installation of a lift, were being planned when I visited it. The dining room, delightfully furnished with pine, has been built on stilts at the back of the premises as the Stour has a nasty habit of flooding in winter. The worst flooding occurred in 1968 when the river entered the home to a depth of eighteen inches. The chapel, the focal point of the home, contains a photograph of the Turin shroud.

On 27th April, 1979, Her Majesty the Queen Mother visited Cavendish by helicopter to open formally the Sue Ryder museum which has been built at the entrance to the Sue Ryder Foundation's headquarters. The Queen Mother in her address said "This museum will not only be a lasting memorial to those who gave their lives in two world wars but also a tangible record of the history and origins of the foundation.

"In a most vivid way this museum reminds us of the human needs which exist in Britain and throughout the world today. We can see here both the struggle and the ultimate triumph of the human spirit in the face of adversity."

It may not be everyone who can face the pictures of horror, destruction and the human carnage of war in the museum, but the beautiful handwork done by the heavily disabled and the dying, the national costumes, the embroidery, the beaten copper work, the model galleon all so painstakingly executed, surely these must be an inspiration to all.

The High Street leads out of the village, following the course of the river eastwards to the *Railway Arms* where it becomes Lower Street. The distinction between High and Lower is not one of elevation but discriminates between the more desirable residential area near the village green and the less fashionable area near the now defunct railway station. This view was confirmed by a group of ladies I chatted to on the village green; they were bitterly complaining about the high rates charged on the property surrounding the green.

A road runs between the *Railway Arms* and the Gatehouse, formerly used by the railway crossing keeper but now a private residence which can boast a station platform as one of its garden accoutrements, and crosses the river by means of the Pentlow Bridge into Essex. Rarely in its upper reaches does the Stour add to the beauty of a village by flowing through its centre. It most frequently skirts the periphery of the village out of sight, keeping most of the dwellings on the Suffolk bank of the river. This is typical of Cavendish where

Sarah Fraser, a shepherdess working at Carlton, near the source of the Stour.

A footbridge carrying the public footpath from Cavendish to Bower Hall across the Stour.

the river flows, obscured from view, along the back of High Street, at one time turning the wheel of Cavendish Mill before disappearing under the Pentlow Bridge.

Good views of the village and the river can be seen by taking the public footpath from the Essex side of Pentlow Bridge to Bower Hall, a sixteenth-century building with a fifteenth-century barn. From this path the village makes a pretty scene, nestled among the trees with its church tower protruding above them, behind which are the regimented rows of vines belonging to the Ambrose vineyard. The path meets the river again near to Bower Hall, where a secluded meadow, quiet beside the Stour, provides an isolated spot on which to park a caravan.

A short distance along the metalled road which leads from Bower Hall, a concrete footpath provides a way across the river and back into the village centre. To attempt to continue the walk from Bower Hall to Clare making use of the course of the old railway line is quite useless, as this has long ago been ploughed into the ground and the bridges taken up.

From beneath Pentlow Bridge the Stour flows round the corner to form

Kenneth Bird in front of his home, Pentlow Hall, which he has restored. The fine oriel window was inserted when the building had an upper floor put in.

part of the moat of Pentlow Hall, which it once completely surrounded. The earliest settlement here was probably a Roman staging post, as Pentlow is on the Roman road from Cambridge through Long Melford and is eleven miles from the former town. Roman staging posts, where horses were changed, were usually between ten and fifteen miles apart.

It is thought the first Hall at Pentlow was built on an island in the river and its chapel, on the site of the present church, was built on the river bank beside it. A freewoman, believed to be a Saxon Abbess from Little Dunmow, first held the manor on behalf of the Church before the Conquest, after which it was one of a hundred and thirty manors given to Ralph Baignard, who resided at Baignard's Castle in Upper Thames Street, London. In 1381 the original Hall, which was twice the size of the present one, was pulled down and thrown into the river by John Wrawe and his followers while on their way to capture Sir John Cavendish at Cavendish.

The present Hall dates from 1475 and has two wings of a later date on each end of the old Hall. Each in turn has been used as the main entrance, which necessitated changing all the internal doors so they hung on the opposite hand. Doors are hung so that they shield the room being entered. The Eastern wing was restored during the reign of Queen Anne and is believed to be an unique example from that period.

Until 1525 the Hall was a single-storey building with a hole in the roof to let the smoke out. At this time the Hall was divided horizontally and the very fine oriel window inserted into the upper storey. The window still contains the original stained glass which depicts a hawking scene, together with heraldic shields associated with the Felton family who resided at the Hall from 1490-1570. Downstairs the walls are lined with very dark linen-fold panelling. Outside, the original plaster is marked with a delicate crow's foot pattern, the trade mark or sign of a Stoke-by-Nayland plasterer. When Kenneth Bird, the present owner, called in the local plasterer to do some restoration work he finished it off with the same crow's foot design, unaware that he was continuing a tradition.

Kenneth Bird, who purchased the Hall in 1966, is working on the

The round tower of Pentlow church, the most northerly church in Essex and one of only six in the county with a round tower.

restoration of the complete building. So far he has lifted the whole Hall section by section to remove the old oak base plates upon which the house stands to replace them with four rows of brickwork. When I spoke to him he was just starting on the delicate task of saving the oriel window.

A mellow, warm-toned bell, installed in the house in 1815 to commemorate the battle of Waterloo, was used by Mrs Bird to call her husband to tea as I left and crossed the moat by means of a rickety old bridge to take the path to the church, which was at one time within the manor grounds.

This church is one of only six in Essex with a round tower, and it is also the most northerly church in this county. Local wags would have you believe that the round tower was originally a well shaft, exposed when the river flooded and washed away the surrounding earth. It would have been a remarkable flood, as the tower is fifty feet high, with walls made from flint and pebble rubble to a thickness of four feet. A more likely explanation is that there was a shortage of suitable building stone with which to form the corner

The tomb of John Kempe and his wife Elinor in Pentlow church. Their children appear on the side of the tomb.

stones of a rectangular tower. The twelfth-century tower, which has fourteenth-century windows, was an addition to the Norman nave.

Saxon churches were frequently dedicated to St Gregory and St George, and as Pentlow church has this dedication it was probably built during the twelfth century on the site of an earlier Saxon church. The apse with its original windows and the west door survive, as does the Norman font, which has a very fine, restored cover decorated with florid wood carving popular in the time of Henry VII. On the north side of the chancel stands a small chapel containing the tomb of Judge George Kempe and that of his son John and John's wife Elinor, who produced fourteen children, commemorated as kneeling figures on the side of the tomb. In a lease of Pentlow Hall to George Kempe on the death of his brother John, their names are listed as Elinor, Elizabeth, Mary, Anne, Margerye, ffranncys, Drewsilla, Tabitha, Bridget, Magdalene, George and John. Presumably the other two boys must have died before their father, who died in 1609.

It is not unusual for a village whose history goes back to medieval times to exist in two parts a mile or so away from each other. Generally the church

The oddly named *Pinkuah Arms* at Pentlow.

marks the position of the earliest settlement, but because of the plague, the soil going sour, the need for fresh water, for reasons of defence or even to avoid being flooded out by the river, the villagers have moved to another site. The exact reason why the villagers of Pentlow decided to move up the hill is uncertain but the modern village is situated at the top of Pentlow Hill. Pen was the name given to a hill by the Celts and later the Saxons used the word Law for the same geographical feature, so today we have Pentlow Hill.

The *Pinkuah Arms* is the unusual name of the village inn, believed to be the only one in England with this name. I was told by the landlord that it could have been named after two sisters, Aggie and Pinkuah Wallace, who lived here during the earlier part of the eighteenth century when the public house was a thatched cottage. A more interesting but less feasible story related to a small boy who ran away from his home in Sudbury and called at the cottage to ask for food. Before obliging, the lady of the house first scrubbed the child clean and on observing her handiwork was heard to remark, "Oh, how pink you are!" Although the building is very old, the *Pinkuah Arms* has held an on-licence for only fifty years. Before that it had only an off-licence and, as Fred Braybrook, the oldest inhabitant, told me, customers drank their beer sitting in the ditch outside until someone provided them with a shed. Today the scene is quite different with mine hosts providing real ale, complemented by home cooking, in a convivial atmosphere under the exposed oak beams.

Bull's tower, a polygonal brick tower ninety feet high, stands on the top of Pentlow Hill, and from its summit on a clear day can be seen forty-eight churches, most of them in Suffolk. It is one of the very few follies to be found in Essex, and was built in 1859 by Edward Bull in memory of his parents, the Reverend John Bull and his wife Margaret, at the spot they loved so much. It is indeed a breath-taking place, with wide panoramic views across a plateau to the north into which has been cut deep valleys by the Stour and its tributaries, the Glem and the Chad Brook.

Genesis Green is an appropriate name for the beginning of a river, although the Glem actually starts half a mile further north at Baxter's Green. As a river is traced back to its source, it divides and sub-divides so many times into numerous tributaries, each having at its head a ditch or a puddle, that it is very difficult to decide on the true source of the river. I had traced the course of the river Glem from where it joins the Stour between Glemsford and Long Melford to Wickhambrook and beyond to Baxter's Green, where I knocked on the door of a pink-washed thatched cottage standing beside the tiny stream. When I asked, "Is this the start of the river Glem" the lady of the house replied, "Well, I've never heard it called that before." When I arrived back at Wickhambrook, by chance I met the local vicar and confided my tale to him. "Ah," he said, drawing on his infinite abundance of wisdom, "my Wickhambrook parishioners know their stream as the Wickham Brook."

This being the case, I followed the Wickham Brook, a tributary of the Glem, from near Genesis Green, six miles directly north of Clare, where Colonel and Mrs Fuller with their son Mark cultivate five acres of Müller Thurgau vines with which to make Genesis wine, through Wickhambrook to Boxted, where the tributary joins the River Glem.

Just south of Genesis Green, set in seventeen acres of parkland, stands Badmondisfield Hall, set back from the road and obscured by its farm buildings. It is reached by crossing a small brick bridge spanning the deeply cut moat, full of fish. The immense size of the Hall is impressive and awe inspiring, but I did not think as picturesque as many of these old Halls. Perhaps this was because its north side, the most pleasant, consisting of brick nogging between oak beams, was in the shadow of the afternoon autumnal sun. Its southern elevation has been bastardised, with modern doors and windows out of keeping with its character. I had seen several pictures and drawings of its Great Baronial Hall (*Suffolk Houses* by Eric Sandon, page 218) but the present owner told me that this had also been drastically altered.

Historically there has been a Hall on this site since the time of Edward the Confessor. Many of its owners since that time have woven their names into the tapestry of our English history. The second Earl of Pembroke, who married King Edward III's fourth daughter, lived here in the fourteenth century. He was defeated by the Spanish during a naval engagement off Rochelle in 1372, was captured and died after a ransom had been paid for his release. Some say he was murdered by poisoning on the way home to England. His son, by his second wife, carried the Golden Spurs at the Coronation of Richard II and married the daughter of John of Gaunt.

Reginald, Lord Grey of Ruthyn and Privy Councillor to Henry IV, lived at Badmondisfield and his son, Sir John, fought in the mud alongside Henry V at the Battle of Agincourt in 1415. At the beginning of the sixteenth century the Hall was purchased by Charles Somerset, Earl of Worcester and Ambassador to France, who attended the extravaganza laid on by Cardinal Wolsey at Ardres, since known as the Field of the Cloth of Gold, in which Henry VIII met King Francis I of France. Wolsey had hoped the outcome would be an alliance between the two countries.

It is believed that Sir George Somerset, the second son of Charles Somerset, built the present Hall some time before he died in 1559. By 1668 the Hall had come into the possession of the Warner family, the first of whom was Francis Warner, Alderman and Sheriff of London. This was at the time of great religious unrest in the country created by Charles II's Corporation Act, Act of Uniformity and the Conventicle Act resulting from an inability to reunite the Puritans to the Church Establishment which revived objections raised in Elizabeth's time. The Queen's first Archbishop, Matthew Parker, lived only a few miles at Stoke by Clare.

Badmondisfield Hall, which was built in the sixteenth century on the site of an earlier hall.

Wickhambrook became a stronghold of Protestant dissenters. A Congregational church was set up in the barn at Badmondisfield Hall, where the chaplains to the Warner household preached to congregations of two hundred or more. One day as the chaplain, Richard Rawlin, left his study, the chimney collapsed into it. As his life had been spared, he took it as an omen that the Lord approved of his work. The Reverend Samuel Cradock is remembered as being the founder of the Congregational church at Wickhambrook and opened his home as an ecclesiastical school for young men.

The intense hatred and intolerance which embittered relations between various religious factions after the Restoration of the Monarchy is vividly described in Edna Lyall's novel *In the Golden Days*—the title is a reference to the reign of Charles II, when life, at least for the privileged, was extravagant, gay and debauched. Edna Lyall, the *nom de plume* of Ada Ellen-Bailey, was an eighteenth-century novelist who lived at Badmondisfield Hall and based her book on the events which had taken place there two centuries earlier, when according to the novel the house belonged to a Colonel Francis Wharncliffe, a religious dissenter and opponent of Charles II. The book has the distinction of being the last one read to the dying Ruskin.

When I entered Wickhambrook flags were flying and crowds cheering for Princess Anne, whose bright red helicopter had touched down on the recreation ground a few minutes before my arrival. The Princess, who is patron of the Horse Riding for the Disabled Association, had come to watch handicapped children display their horsemanship at the Hill View riding stables. It was the first time in sixty-seven years that a member of the Royal Family had set foot in this remote corner of Suffolk, the previous occasion being 17th September, 1912, when King George V visited the village.

Wickhambrook, they say, is ten miles from anywhere. It is the most spread-out village in Suffolk, being five miles across and containing no fewer than eleven village greens. It evolved from an amalgamation of a number of scattered hamlets which had been set up by peasants trying to escape from the plague. It was not unusual for a stricken village to be abandoned and a fresh community started a short distance away.

Of several medieval Halls in this district, Gifford's Hall standing on the hill just below the riding school, off the Bury to Haverhill road, is one of the finest and most picturesque examples of a fifteenth-century house remaining in England. At one stage it was nearly lost to Wickhambrook when it was proposed to take it down and re-erect it in the Victoria and Albert Museum, London. The Hall takes its name from Peter Gifford, owner of the original Hall on this site at the time of Edward I. It belonged to Sir Thomas Heigham in Elizabeth's reign. He was an officer in her army who fought in Ireland with great distinction at Clein Castle and defeated the Irish at Blackwater, to the delight of his queen.

I left the people of Wickhambrook rejoicing over their Royal visit and continued my journey downstream to discover Denston. The unexpected is always more delightful than the anticipated, and as I turned right, over the little bridge beside Bridge Cottage, pink washed and thatched, and drove to the top of the hill to enter Denston Green, I found it to be truly a pretty place.

From the tiny triangular green dominated by the war memorial a row of immaculately kept white thatched cottages descends the hill to the gates of Denston Hall, an eighteenth-century red-brick house. A Tudor farmhouse and the fourteenth-century church in the late Perpendicular style stand at the top of the green, from which there are panoramic views of the surrounding countryside.

A chantry college was founded here in 1475 by the Denston family to sing the mass and to offer prayers for their departed souls. Towards the end of the

White-walled thatched cottages on the edge of Denston Green.

fourteenth century wealthy people were no longer moved to bequeath their worldly goods for the construction of new churches. Instead they left their money to a priest or priests who would sing the mass and say prayers for them and their named friends. The bequest was in the form of an endowment which would provide funds in perpetuity for the chantry. Small chapels were often built within the existing churches in which the mass was chanted.

From Denston the open country road winds its way across the top of an exposed gently sloping plateau across a watershed into the next valley in which lies the village of Hawkedon. Here the V-shaped valley is steep and the stream, dry in summer, crosses the country road to Glemsford.

From the fifteenth-century church, isolated from the neighbouring farmhouse and dwellings by an expansive green, the road descends rapidly to follow the river along the bottom of a steep wooded valley to Boxted—not to be confused with the Boxted in Essex, which lies in the Stour valley east of

The Hartest stone, a mysterious survival from the Ice Ages which is said to have been fetched from the next parish in the eighteenth century.

Nayland. Here another tributary flowing from Hartest, a mile to the north, joins our stream to form the River Glem, which now flows south to join the Stour.

Hartest is a delightfully unspoilt village surrounding the now characteristic three-sided green, on which a couple of goats had been tethered to keep down the grass. The church stands at the bottom of the green near to the river, and here in the churchyard an enterprising vicar had employed some sheep and a couple of geese to keep down the grass and the weeds.

The *Crown Inn* is strategically placed next to the church and was once used as the meeting place of the Manor Court. It has now been restored but retains its original Jacobean wood panelling in the lounge bar. At the top of the green remote from the church can be found a large Ice-Age boulder stone. It measures about four foot across and is about two foot high. How it arrived there is something of a mystery.

According to history the people of Hartest were so overjoyed by the signing of the Treaty of Utrecht in 1713 that they decided to celebrate the event by harnessing more than forty horses to a sledge on to which they loaded the stone and, placing a trumpeter on top of it, ceremonially dragged the stone a mile from a field in Somerton, the next parish, to its present position at the top corner of the village green in Hartest. Some say the stone was moved to celebrate Marlborough's victories, but if so the celebrations were a little late as the stone was moved in August, 1714, and Marlborough's last battle took place in 1709. George I ascended the English throne in 1714, so the stone could have been placed in position to mark this event. From 1789 until 1959 on St George's Day a fair with merry making took place on Hartest green on the anniversary of George III's visit to St Paul's Cathedral to give thanks for his recovery from an illness.

Personally I don't think the stone was moved to celebrate anything. For one thing, if it was moved for this purpose, why was it left at the top of the green and not brought down to the church, erected in a place of honour, or even placed next door to serve as a beer table at the *Crown Inn*? In my opinion it just grew there where it now stands! Perhaps a woman or child returning from the fields, where they earned a copper or two stone picking, absent-mindedly tossed a stone away, the conditions were favourable and it grew!

My theory that the stone grew* where it now stands is equally as probable as the local legend at Hartest, which would have us believe that the stone turns over—or is it round?—when it hears the church clock strike midnight.

My first instinct, induced by an unsightly transformer with its attendant electrical cables stretched across the road, was to hurry through Boxted, but its charming arboreal parkland and a sign which pointed across the river to its church persuaded me to stay and investigate. If Kedington church is the Westminster Abbey of Suffolk, then the monuments to the Poley family, who have occupied Boxted Hall since the fifteenth century, make this prim little church of All Saints resemble a miniature St Paul's Cathedral. The black effigies of William and Alice Poley, the latter with a dog at her feet, are made from wood rather than the normal marble or alabaster. Danish visitors to the church will be particularly interested in the memorial to Sir John Poley, who died in 1638, and the adjacent one erected to the memory of his wife Abigail, who died fourteen years later. Sir John Poley was a professional soldier, who for twenty years served in the Danish army fighting for King Christian of Denmark, with whom he was great friends. He reached the rank of Colonel-General, and was awarded the Order of the Elephant, the highest order of

*Another Suffolk village, Blaxhall, has a stone that grows, according to tradition.

chivalry in Denmark and second oldest in Europe. Its emblem is a small gold frog worn as an earring.* Both Sir Winston Churchill and Prince Charles were made members of this Order.

Glemsford is situated on the top of a hill of boulder clay 275 feet high. Iceberg-like, the clay goes down to a depth of 300 feet below sea level, making it the deepest seam of boulder clay in England. The town has commanding views of the Glem valley as its river winds its way south from Boxted to join the Stour a mile to the south-east of the village.

The road to Glemsford leaves the Glem after crossing it at Scotch Ford bridge to wend its way up the hill past a delightful old Hall, built in 1614 during the reign of James I, to the church; a fine example of Perpendicular architecture built with the profits from the "Old Draperies". The benefactor was John Golding, clothmaker and member of a wealthy family of wool merchants, who died in 1496. The church may not be as lavish as Lavenham or have the panache of Melford, but some devoted Christian souls have gone down on their knees to give it polished floors which outshine all others.

The discovery of worked flints at Glemsford dates man's occupation of this hill from Neolithic times. At least three different tribes of Celtic origin lived here in the Iron Age, and came under the influence of the Druid priests, who were known to have had their grove or lodge at Glemsford. Later in Roman times some of the Iceni settled on the hill and K. W. Glass in his *History of Glemsford* speculates that Boudica could have come from one of their number. It may have been the Romans who gave Glemsford the name Little Egypt by which Glemsford is still known locally, because of the number of priests in the locality. On the other hand it may be a survival from medieval times when the people on the hill kept themselves aloof from the busy commercial trade going on in the Stour valley below.

Glemsford has been associated with textiles ever since the Bayeux tapestry was reputedly made here by English needlewomen. Although there is no absolute proof of this, it is known that the manor of Guthelnesford (Glemsford) belonged in 1086 to Adeliza, wife of Bishop Odo, William the Conqueror's half-brother, who ordered the Bayeux tapestry, which depicts the decline and fall of King Harold, to be made and for it to be hung in Bayeux cathedral, Normandy.

The village was at its most prosperous during the time of the "Old Draperies" in the fifteenth century, when all the Stour towns and villages were busily engaged in making the coarse broadcloth and Glemsford its own special Gleynforth. The next century saw the decline of this industry and the introduction of the manufacture of new finer cloth from Holland, the "New Draperies", did nothing to halt the increasing poverty in the wool towns. By the end of the seventeenth century Suffolk was the twelfth poorest county in the country.

*The elephant and the frog represent the largest and smallest quadrupeds.

It was about this time that the wealthy ceased to make their money over to chantries, as at Denston, but left it instead for the relief of the poor. Several of these charities were amalgamated to form the Glemsford United Charities.

The passing of the Spitalfields Act of 1774 seems to have encouraged the London silk manufacturers to set up their factories outside London, and so in 1824 cheap labour, unemployment and the weaving skills of its workers brought silk to Glemsford. Silk was one of several imported materials which had helped to bring about the decline of the home woollen industry. A silk throwing mill was established at Glemsford in 1824, to take raw silk imported from China and Japan and by winding, doubling, twisting and spinning produce a silk thread ready for dyeing and weaving. It was this factory which spun the thread used by Warners of Braintree and Walters of Sudbury to weave the material for the Coronation dress of Queen Elizabeth II. Glemsford silk was also used for the Investiture robes of Charles, Prince of Wales, and Princess Anne's wedding dress.

Workers were once summoned to the factory by a 75-pound bell hung outside the works, which was rung three minutes before starting time. Latecomers were fined one half penny for each session they were late.

Children playing in the Stour near Glemsford.

Coconut mat weaving became popular during the nineteenth century when no fewer than ten factories were set up at Glemsford to weave the fibres, known as coir and found in the outer husks of the coconut, into matting. In 1906 the village produced what was then the largest carpet in the world. Covering 63,000 square feet, it was transported to London by train and then carried in a convoy, a mile long, containing thirty-seven of Harrods' pantechnicons to Olympia where it was used as a floor covering.

Horse hair sofas were very popular in the Victorian era and of the many factories existing at this time in Glemsford to treat horse hair that of Arnold & Gould, established in 1907, is now the only factory in the country which

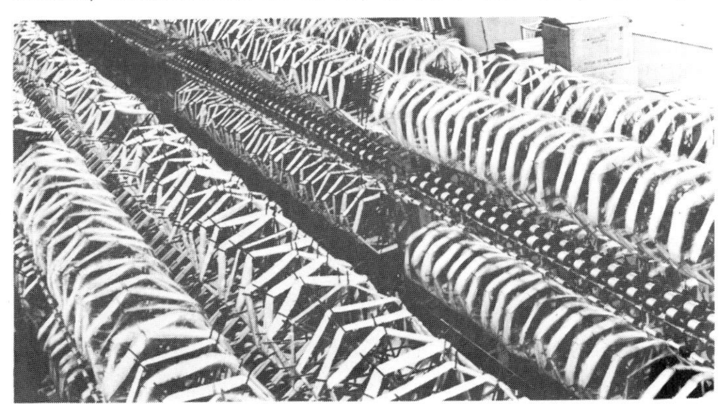

Winding silk at the Glemsford silk factory.

supplies horse hair for the manufacture of brushes, inter linings for clothing, violin bows and blinds for railway carriages. Raw hair, which comes from all parts of the world including both the Americas, Australia, Russia and Mongolia, is pulled wet through vertical combs, which cleans, straightens and disentangles the hair, a process known as wet hackling. The hair is then dry hackled and finished off by double drawing. Hair of the same length is made up into locks and bundles but hair too short for drawing is sent for curling and then used for stuffing mattresses and furniture. At one time there were also horse hair factories at Lavenham, Hadleigh and Long Melford.

Another Glemsford industry, which has its roots in the textile industry and still flourishes, is engineering, represented by the firm of E. W. Downs. Ernest Downs was the village blacksmith way back in 1850 and in 1887 formed the firm of Downs and Smith to make machinery required for the weaving of coconut matting. Now they make machinery for grading and handling potatoes which is exported worldwide.

Before taking the third of its right-angle bends to flow south again, the Stour passes through the grounds of the Cannon Rubber factory, makers of rubber mats, plastic household equipment and babies' plastic feeding bottles. A flax factory originally occupied this site.

CHAPTER FOUR

Long Melford to Sudbury and the Chad Brook

THE CHAD Brook rises in the village of Rede, near the highest point in Suffolk, 427 feet above sea level. It drains the same watershed, coinciding roughly with the main Haverhill to Bury St Edmunds road (the A143), as the River Glem to the west and the River Brett to the east, all three rivers flowing parallel in a south-easterly direction to join the Stour.

Rede church overlooks the beginning of the Chad Brook in its shallow valley, no more than an indentation in the ground at this point. Behind the church and a little distance from it across the road stands the village green, around which is grouped the old school house, the pond and the *Plough Inn*, whose buildings, originally three cottages, date back to the sixteenth century. It is a pity the sources of all rivers and their tributaries are not clearly marked with an old English public house, standing beside their headstream. It would make the geography easier and seeking them out irresistible!

The ground here is high, exposed and treeless, but the Chad valley soon deepens into the characteristic V-shape and, having passed through the grounds of Brockley Hall, the brook flows into Chadacre park, typical English sylvan parkland in which stands Chadacre Hall. Built in the Georgian style about 1834, it was the home of Lord Halifax, but since 1921 it has formed part of the Chadacre Agricultural Institute. The First Earl of Iveagh purchased the Hall and the estate in 1918 and set up a trust fund to establish and endow an Institute for agricultural training, which opened in 1921. Besides the Hall, the Institute comprises a modern well-equipped teaching building, the farm training centre, and three adjoining farms with a herd of pedigree Friesian dairy cows, a herd of Landrace sows and a flock of ewes for fat lamb production.

Students between seventeen and eighteen years of age, who have already worked on a farm for a year, attend the residential college for two winters, spending the intervening summer on a commercial farm. At the end of the course, which trains the students to be stockmen or general farm assistants, and eventually to become foremen or farm managers, successful students are awarded the Chadacre Certificate and the National Certificate of Agriculture.

Having passed through Chadacre, the Chad Brook continues through Shimpling as if to join the Brett near to the medieval town of Lavenham, but having flowed underneath the A134, Sudbury to Bury St Edmunds road at

Bridge Street, it changes its mind and turns to flow past Melford Hall. At Long Melford the brook was once diverted to feed the ancient watermill, whose mill house still exists beside the bridge, which replaced the mill ford giving the name Melford to the village, before it joins the Stour.

Melford Hall, complete with pepper pot turrets towering above the perimeter wall which lines the eastern boundary of the village green, is typical of the red brick Tudor buildings constructed towards the end of the reign of Henry VIII. It was built with local bricks made from clay dug from near the village green, a spot now known as claypits pond, and constructed on the site of an earlier Hall, parts of which were incorporated into the present building.

From the time of Edward the Confessor the Melford estate belonged to the Abbots at Bury St Edmunds until confiscated at the Dissolution of the Monasteries by Henry VIII and given to an ambitious lawyer, William Cordell. In Queen Mary's reign he was knighted, appointed Solicitor-General, Speaker of the House of Commons and Master of the Rolls. He was sufficiently resourceful to be able to continue in these offices when Elizabeth came to the throne. Cordell completed his new mansion somewhere between 1554 and 1560, in sufficient time to entertain Queen Elizabeth when she visited Long Melford in 1578.

Queen Anne Boleyn had earlier been entertained at Melford Place, a Tudor mansion at the other end of the street.

Melford Hall is now the home of Sir Richard Hyde Parker, twelfth Baronet and Lord of the Manor of Melford, who talked to me in his study about the history of the Hall and his family's association with it. He told me that Melford Hall was purchased in 1786 by Sir Harry Parker with some of the family fortune his father, Sir Hyde Parker (1714-82), Vice-Admiral of the Blue, had amassed from Prize money awarded to him whilst he was in the navy. After an act of 1708 an English ship capturing an enemy craft could claim it as prize and the value of vessel and cargo was assessed. The money was then distributed between the officers and men, it being apportioned according to rank. This was an incentive to recruitment and resulted in enemy ships being captured rather than sunk. A Captain in 1799 obtained about £40,000, a fortune by any standards, and the seamen were awarded about £200, nearly fourteen years' pay for them.

The fifth Baronet would have accumulated another fortune when he circumnavigated the globe with Commodore Anson's squadron in 1740-44. The purpose of the mission was primarily to attack the Spanish ports along the west coast of South America from the Pacific ocean. To a considerable extent the squadron was manned with pensioners from Greenwich Hospital. Anson and Hyde Parker set out in the *Centurion* accompanied by five other ships, none of which returned, and although the military objective of the mission came to nothing, they captured the Spanish treasure ship, *Nuestra Senora de*

Covadonga of the Philippines with a half million pounds worth of treasure on board. Four years after its departure, the *Centurion* returned to England in 1744, having circumnavigated the globe and having had the distinction of being the first English warship to have visited China.

When Admiral Byron returned to England due to ill health Hyde Parker succeeded him as Commander in chief of the West Indies. Later he commanded a fleet in the North Sea, fought the Dutch off the Dogger Bank in 1781, and then joined the East India Command in his ship *Cato* and was lost at sea.

His younger son (1739-1807), also a Vice-Admiral, commanded the English fleet at Copenhagen in 1801, and sent the famous signal to Horatio

The Long Melford village sign.

Nelson, his second-in-command, reading "Leave Off Action" which Nelson chose to ignore. Placing his telescope to his blind eye, Nelson commented, "I really do not see the signal."

Although the fifth Baronet is rightly considered to be the first and finest Admiral of the Parker family, recent delving into the family archives, I was told, has uncovered another family seafarer at the time of Drake, who also plundered Spanish ships on the high seas in acts of piracy and won for his queen, Elizabeth, and himself a fortune in gold.

The first Baronet, who came to London from the family seat at North Moulton in Devon, was honoured with his hereditary title for services to the City of London, probably in lieu of being appointed Lord Mayor, a title which involved considerable expense. Sir Richard, the present Baronet, is the twelfth member of the family to succeed to the title. He was educated at Millfield

School and after serving in the Army he attended the Royal Agricultural College at Cirencester, and now farms two thousand acres of the three-thousand-acre estate, on which are grown cereal crops and sugar beet. In 1972 he married Elizabeth Leslie, of Otten Hall, just down the river from Melford.

Their private apartments within the Hall are decorated and furnished in a contemporary fashion in marked contrast to the sombre, dark oak linenfold panelling of the banqueting hall. Their drawing room in the East Wing is light in contrast, with a stone floor and decorated in white or near white with similar coloured furnishings. Sir Richard's private study, also light and spacious, reflects his taste in modern painting and fine art, particularly Chinese porcelain and ivory. He particularly likes some of the work of the painter Nick Evans, referred to as the "Van Gogh of the coalminers", whose pictures in monochrome depicting the conditions of miners underground blend tastefully with more traditional works. He also admires the work of the painter Euan Uglow and that of the sculptor Ivor Roberts-Jones.

From the medieval solemnity of the main banqueting hall, open to the public, a grand staircase surmounted by a double row of Ionic columns supporting a segmental coved ceiling leads to the gallery which contains a stained glass window featuring Queen Elizabeth I and commemorating her visit to the Hall. There is also a portrait of Countess Rivers, who for a while owned the mansion. Unlike William Cordell, its first owner, she remained loyal to her Catholic faith and, being a Royalist, had her home ransacked during the Civil War. She, poor lady, died in a London debtor's prison. When the present Baronet's father died Melford Hall was surrendered to the Treasury in part payment of death duties and it now belongs to the National Trust, leaving Sir Richard a tenant in his ancestral home.

Beatrix Potter, the well-known author and illustrator of children's books, was related to the Hyde Parker family and a regular guest at Melford Hall, where she did many water colour paintings, both of the Hall and of her favourite animals. These paintings are now exhibited at Melford Hall in rooms which she occupied during her visits.

It is a pity that an Englishman's home is no longer his castle, but happily Sir Richard has a keen sense of history and a deep commitment to the preservation of the English heritage of which he is part.

Long Melford was a Roman staging point from which led five Roman roads, the main two following the Stour valley west to Cambridge and the other at right angles, linking Colchester with Bury St Edmunds to the north. Several ingenious methods have been used to discover these roads, including the use of a water diviner and aerial photography from a radio-controlled model aircraft which revealed a hidden track running north to south across the

The pepper-pot turrets of Melford Hall. ▶

village green. In 1958 a fine, tessellated Roman pavement was found in Melford Place Park while sewer pipes were being buried.

Like most of the Stour villages, Long Melford derived its wealth from wool but unlike the others managed to retain it well into the eighteenth century. Its past prosperity is evident in the fine property surrounding its spacious village green, undoubtedly the most impressive in the Stour valley.

Ernest Ambrose was born in 1878 in a cottage at the top of the green in Church Row. At the age of ninety-six he related to his wife Emma stories of his youth and of his life by the village green, which she set down in a book, *Melford Memories*. It is a remarkable work ranking, in my opinion, with Ronald Blythe's best-seller, *Akenfield*, but better in that it is a first-hand account of village life at the turn of the century.

As I emerged from Melford Hall and stood in its brick gateway by an ornate octagonal summerhouse and looked across the village green, I tried to recall those scenes so vividly described by Ernest Ambrose. It is incredible how life has changed within one man's lifetime. Today there is a continuous stream of cars, lorries and massive juggernauts hurrying across the green; but barely seventy years ago horses still provided the only reliable form of transport.

The roads were no more than farm tracks with large pot-holes occasionally filled in by women and children with stones they had picked from the fields for twopence a bushel. Gentlemen rode on horseback or in fine carriages drawn by four horses, with a coachman and footman sitting on top resplendent in their colourful uniforms. Farmers and tradesmen drove round in gigs or buggies brandishing their long whips, while young ladies drove or were driven round in

small carriages, and even the local bus to Sudbury market was horsedrawn.

It is, however, the car which has made these country villages accessible and brought them renewed prosperity from the tourist industry. There were many more characters about the green in those days before the first world war; the bag man who sold ribbons and laces and all things pretty for the ladies; the tea man who dispensed tea at sixpence a quarter; the appleman, who cried, "Come and buy me apples-O"; and the sandman who supplied a fine white silver sand for sprinkling on the rough earth or stone cottage floors to keep them clean. There were the entertainers scraping an honest living by amusing the passers-by, such as the man with his performing bear, the organ grinder with his friendly monkey, the German bands blasting out Gilbert and Sullivan, the travelling menagerie and the strolling players who performed their dramas in the village hall. They have now been replaced by television, which keeps people indoors, apart from one another, so that they have lost the art of rhetoric and the ability to amuse and entertain themselves.

Then there was the great annual fair held on the village green, whose main business was the trading of horses together with their tackle and trappings but which also provided the only holiday that people had in those days. There was much merry-making, drunkenness and brawling, particularly between the fair men and the gypsies whose gaily painted caravans added colour to the scene. The swings and roundabouts, operated by horses which trotted round in a circle, were placed at the top of the green. The horses were soon replaced by steam engines, which also operated the steam organs that gave the familiar fairground sound, far superior to the canned "pop" of today.

◀ Sir Richard Hyde Parker's light modern private drawing room at Melford Hall, contrasting strongly with the sombre colouring of most other rooms.

Dark panelling gives this room at Melford Hall a totally different appearance from Sir Richard's own apartments.

On the green opposite the entrance to the Hall stands a four-hundred-year-old conduit, a medieval brickwork structure covering a spring which once supplied the water for Melford Hall through wooden pipes cut from elm. Rare cuckoo flowers still grow round its base. The grass here is left uncut to preserve them.

Overlooking the village and the green from its highest point is the Hospital of the Holy and Blessed Trinity, a charitable institution for old and destitute villagers founded by Sir William Cordell in 1573; a Royal Charter was proclaimed in 1591. In his will of 1580 Sir William left sufficient funds to allow the pensioners 13 pence (5½p) a week, later raised to 16 pence (7p), and the warden ten shillings (50p) a week.

The red brick building surrounded by a high wall built in 1633 unfortunately obscures the view of the church from the green. Sir William was forced to place his hospital in this position because the more suitable site further to the east belonged to Kentwell Hall, and as the owners were not on speaking terms at the time Sir William was obliged to build on his own land in front of the church. On Sundays the tenants marched to church in single file wearing long black cloaks and top hats. As Ernest Ambrose recalled in his book *Melford Memories*, "The warden led the way looking very important, with an elegant black-striped shoulder cape over his cloak and a thick cord with big tassels to tie it with, to show his authority."

The hospital has recently been modernised and now consists of thirteen self-contained flats, seven of them double rooms, in which the elderly can live rent free. It is one of the finest almshouses in the country.

The Church of the Holy Trinity is considered along with its neighbour at Lavenham to be, architecturally, among the best of its period in the country. Pevsner* describes Melford church as "large, proud and noble." Particularly impressive is the nave, 153 feet long, lit by tall transomed clerestory windows towering above the three-light windows in each bay.

The original tower was destroyed by lightning in 1710, being replaced by an ugly square red-brick tower covered in cement. This was replaced at the beginning of this century by the present elegant tower built, at least in part, to celebrate Queen Victoria's diamond jubilee. The tower was completed in 1903 and the four pinnacles on the top of the 118 foot tower were named Victoria, Edward, Alexandra and Martyn, after the late Queen and her successor King Edward VII with his Queen Alexandra and Charles Martyn, the rector at that time.

Inside the church the reredos behind the high altar is made from Caen stone but this is modern being given in 1877 by the mother of Charles Martyn. To the right of the altar is the tomb of Sir William Cordell and on the left that of John Clopton, a member of the family who owned Kentwell Hall.

This sixteenth-century manor lies to the north of Melford Green and is

*_Buildings of England — Suffolk._

"Large, proud and noble" is Nikolaus Pevsner's description of Long Melford church, seen here from within the churchyard.

approached from the main road to Bury St Edmunds through an avenue three quarters of a mile long, containing 250 pollarded lime trees. These were planted by Sir Thomas Robinson, protonotary, a chief clerk or registrar, to the Court of Common Pleas, who had purchased the Hall in 1678. Unfortunately he did not live long enough to enjoy his handiwork, for in 1683 he died jumping from a window of his Chambers at the Inns of Court in an attempt to escape from a fire.

The trees were nearly destroyed when a later owner decided to sell the limes to a London piano manufacturer, but happily they were bought back at great cost, although not before some had been felled. The remainder of this majestic avenue of trees is still there today. The present red-brick Elizabethan moated manor was built by Sir William Clopton before 1560 near another mansion, a quarter of a mile away, known as the Lutons, which was pulled down after the completion of the present manor.

At the time of Domesday the estate belonged to the Abbot of Bury, whose brother Trodo occupied it, as did his descendants the de Kentwells until it passed to the Crown for a period. It was then leased to a number of people until in 1379, according to Copinger*, "Sir John Cobham and others obtained a licence to grant the manor to Katharine, the wife of Sir Thomas Clopton." There is also a suggestion that the manor was first granted to Katharine's father, William de Mylde, but however that might be, it did pass to Thomas and Katharine's son William Clopton, who died in 1446. When Sir Thomas Clopton died his wife Katharine married Sir William Tendring. Her daughter by this second marriage, Alice, married Sir John Howard (1398) and had a grandson who became the first Duke of Norfolk; his descendants included Queen Elizabeth I and Catherine Howard.

Sir William Clopton, died 1562, the builder of the present Hall, was the last male person of that name to occupy the manor. His daughter Anne, educated by Lady Anne Barnardiston at Clare Priory, was only seven when she was introduced to Sir Simonds D'Ewes, and they married when she was thirteen. Although she seems to have been perpetually pregnant during her marriage, only one daughter, Cecilia, survived infancy. Anne Clopton died of smallpox at the early age of twenty-nine, a miserable pattern of life common to most women at this time. Cecilia married Sir Thomas Darcy, but as there was no heir from this marriage the estate was sold to Sir Thomas Robinson.

Today Kentwell Hall is owned by Patrick Phillips, a barrister who has purchased the Hall along with fifty acres of its land. He and his wife Judith have set about restoring the building without Government aid, raising the money by making the Hall available for social functions, medieval banquets, etc., and opening it to the public. It is a mammoth task to undertake.

Long Melford is so described because of its High Street being over a mile from end to end. It is also one of the widest streets in the county. Starting at the bottom of Melford Green by the red-brick Victorian school, built by Sir William Parker in 1860 in a similar style to Melford Hall, the High Street crosses the Chad Brook to pass in front of the *Bull Hotel*, a very fine timber-framed fifteenth-century building. For many years its splendid oak beams were hidden behind a Georgian facade, which was not removed until 1935 when the original Tudor front was revealed and dated as c 1540.

The premises were originally the home of a prosperous wool merchant and contained warehouses and workshops as well as his residence. By 1580 the *Bull* had become an inn, just in time for its customers to toast the arrival of

*Copinger. *Manors of Suffolk.*

Queen Elizabeth I in a stained glass window at Melford Hall.

Queen Elizabeth I in the town. Soon afterwards, in 1613, the Drew family became the landlords and remained until the eighteenth century, when Charles Drew murdered his father at the inn and as a result the family estates were confiscated. During the Civil War in 1648 another murder had taken place at the *Bull* when a wealthy Melford yeoman, Richard Evered, was attacked and killed by Roger Grene in the doorway.

I have fond memories of the *Bull* as I stayed there with my family to escape from demanding boys and doting parents when I was a boarding school housemaster. We used to sink into deep armchairs in front of a blazing log fire contained within a massive hearthplace measuring twelve feet across, still with its original Elizabethan brickwork and chimney stack, to take afternoon tea. It was the custom in those days to place daintily cut sandwiches on a silver salver in the middle of the room from which guests were invited to help themselves, the salver being replenished at frequent intervals. The invitation to "eat one's fill" certainly added to the hospitality and warmth of the place.

Long Melford High Street can be recommended for the excellence and variety of its eating places, which cater for every pocket and occasion.

Hanging on the wall by the bar in the *Crown* is a framed plaque on which is described the rioting which took place in Melford High Street during polling day in the General Election held on the 1st December, 1885. This was the first occasion that the electoral roll included all male householders, and the newly enfranchised voters were intent on exercising their rights. Unfortunately the people of Glemsford, mainly Liberal, were required to walk the four and a half miles to Long Melford, in Tory territory, to register their votes, which meant they lost a day's work and therefore a day's pay. Having recorded their votes they expressed their dissatisfaction by smashing windows in the town and ransacking the *Crown*.

A timetable of the day's events went as follows:

10.00 a.m. 400 voters assemble at Glemsford and march in a column to Long Melford, led on horseback by factory manager Henry Cook, known as "Captain" Cook.

1.00 p.m. Having recorded their votes they jeer at the police and throw stones at them, then rampage through High Street smashing windows, poking out the upper-storey windows with poles.

3.00 p.m. Riot Act read outside Melford Police Station by a local magistrate standing on a barrel, and being pelted with flour bags for his trouble. After this anyone remaining in the street was liable to arrest.

Looting of public houses now takes place, the *Crown* being completely sacked. One man "found dead" in the cellar was later diagnosed as being only dead drunk.

6.00 p.m. Twenty soldiers arrive from Bury barracks. One of the rioters, "Long Jack", threatens them with his bare hands.

The order "Fix bayonets" is given. Police draw truncheons and form up in front of troops. Rioters retreat in front of advancing line of police, flee across the Green and escape into the fields.

Six weeks later Henry "Captain" Cook stood trial with a dozen other rioters, but they were acquitted. This was the last time that the Riot Act was read in Suffolk.

Half way down Melford High Street one can turn off into a country lane squeezing itself unobtrusively between two shops. This leads to Liston church, a fine building with a red-brick Tudor tower and a Norman nave. On its way to the church the lane runs parallel with one of the prettiest reaches of the river Stour. Here, by the white-boarded mill house on the Essex bank, is a favourite place for fishing, a picnic or just a stroll along the river bank. Just above this point the Chad Brook, having flowed across the Melford meadows, joins the Stour. As I sat on the river bank I found it hard to believe that less than a mile away upstream was a modern flavour factory straddling the river.

I first learnt of the existence of the factory when I talked to a lady in Liston church while she was tidying it up, how well these devoted ladies look after our churches, and she told me that as a little girl she would pick flowers while out walking and hand them in at the factory gate in return for a few pennies pocket money. A modest sign which read "Bush Boake Allen" pointed the way down a narrow country lane to an up-to-date factory entrance flourishing stern warnings about unauthorised entry. When I asked an old man, who was digging his garden opposite, what they made over there, he replied knowingly, "Everything."

An answer which turned out to be particularly accurate, if rather uninformative, as I found out when I was later shown round the factory by George Burnett, the factory manager, accompanied by Raymond Black of Bush Boake Allen. The primary purpose of the firm is to extract those minute quantities of chemicals, essences, essential oils and spice extracts contained in plants, vegetables and fruits which impart to them their characteristic flavours and fragrance, used in cooking to add taste and relish to a choice dish.

To this factory in a quiet bend of the river Stour come raw materials from every part of the world. Buchu leaves from South Africa contain an oil which is the basis of blackcurrant flavours used in beverages and confectionery; bay leaves from Turkey provide the flavour for chicken dishes; durian flavour is shipped from Malaysia to be used in toothpaste, drinks and sweets—the fruit with its characteristic taste is very popular in Malaysia; allspice comes from the dried unripe fruit of the West Indian pimento tree; and the extract from Kola nuts from West Africa is used in Cola drinks. Onions from Egypt, oranges from California, lemons from Sicily, Cardamom fruits from the Himalayas and vanilla from Mauritius are all made to release their vital ingredients at Long Melford.

This is achieved in one of three ways. The essential ingredients may first be dissolved out of the material using a solvent such as an alcohol, usually isopropyl alcohol. Secondly, they may be boiled out with water, the steam carrying with it the volatile aromatic vapours, which are made liquid again by distillation. Thirdly, fractional distillation is used, a process which separates a mixture of liquids into its components by passing their vapours up a tall column. As the vapours ascend the column they cool and those with the higher boiling point condense first and are thus separated from those liquids with lower boiling points which condense further up the column.

The processing rooms contain a veritable array of boilers, cauldrons, and glass tubes. And condensers through which the cooling water from the Stour flows reach up to the ceiling, supported within a metallic framework. There is very little action to see or hear, apart from the constant slow drip of the precious quintessence into its receiver.

The three warehouses at Melford contain over 3,000 tons of different spices, the largest collection in Britain, from which are made at least thirty-five different curry powders as well as a variety of seasonings for commercially made food products, sausages, hamburgers, beefburgers, and baconburgers, each one blended to the food manufacturers' specification. Caraway seeds are brought from Holland, cinnamon from Sri Lanka, celery seeds from India, cloves from Zanzibar, coriander seeds from Russia, garlics from Spain, ginger root from Jamaica, nutmegs from the East and West Indies and pepper from Sarawak.

The "hotness" of a curry is controlled by the quantities of mustard, ginger, pepper and chilli, cayenne pepper made from the pod of the capsicum. Black pepper comes from the dried immature berries of the Piper nigrum, which I was told is left out in the Indian sun to dry in the villages, where people and animals walk over it. To convert the black to white pepper in these villages it is thrown into water, where the outer shell is soaked off and the seed dried. Spice extracts, having been processed at Melford, contain no harmful bacteria.

By using carefully blended spice extracts, instead of the natural spices, whose exact composition can vary because of the vagaries of the weather while it is growing or for some other reason, the food manufacturer can guarantee the consistency of quality, flavour and fragrance of his product. The blending of spice extracts also allows him to order a particular mixture to suit the individual palate of his customers.

The reader may by now be wondering how a modern flavour factory came to be situated in the heart of the East Anglian countryside. On this site during the eighteenth century stood Liston Mill, drawing power from the Stour with which to manufacture paper. At the beginning of the next century the mill was converted into a flax works, of which there were several along the river at this time, the crop being grown locally and the river water used for retting or soaking the bundles of flax. Flax continued to be processed here until 1899.

The firm of Stafford Allen & Sons, of Ampthill in Bedfordshire, purchased the mill and much of the surrounding farm land, for the cultivation of medicinal herbs, in 1899. At first the factory extracted the essential oils from locally grown crops of lavender, peppermint, rosemary, chamomile and dill, but as the demand for their products, both pharmaceutical and perfumery, increased they gradually turned to imported raw materials.

Chlorophyll, the green colouring matter in plants, has been extracted at Melford for more than fifty years, first from locally grown nettles, now from grass brought from Norfolk. The grass meal left after the extraction of the chlorophyll is sold as cattle food. At one time the firm kept a herd of Large White pigs which it fed on the waste from the factory. Chlorophyll is used in such products as toothpaste as a deodorant.

In 1966 the firm of Stafford Allen, with their head office at Islington, North London, merged with two others to form the present company of Bush Boake Allen, which is one of four divisions within the Albright and Wilson Group. The local firm still maintains its interest in pharmaceutical products, manufacturing camphorated opium tinctures for use in cough mixtures,

Distillation towers in the Bush Boake Allen factory. Water from the Stour provides cooling. ▶

which are also completed on the premises, Friars Balsam, liquorice extracts from Russian imported root, and Kaolin Morphine mixtures for upset stomachs. It is also the largest exporter of perfumes in the country, mainly to Africa where they sell a perfume with the unromantic title, to the English ear, of "Bint El Sudan," with body lotions and talcum powder to match.

The firm imports from Iran frankincense and myrrh, from which is extracted an oil to use as a fixative for their expensive range of perfumes. As I left the factory, my guide George Burnett commented in his deep Scottish accent, "We have the frankincense and myrrh, all we need now is the gold," and my parting shot to him was "and I bet given a chance you would extract something from that rather than bury it in the ground."

The old man at the cottage opposite the factory had said to me, "They make everything over there". He was not far wrong.

The Stour meanders slowly away from the factory in three sweeping curves through the meadows behind Melford's long street, taking up the waters of the Chad Brook before it once again comes into public view at Rodbridge corner. Here the county council has made a most attractive picnic spot by landscaping with trees and shrubs the flooded gravel pits beside the Stour. From here the old railway track has been converted into the "Valley Walk," a path which pedestrians can take to Sudbury, passing Borley mill to meet the Stour again at Brundon mill, from where the river can be followed to the mill at Sudbury. The lack of contamination by agricultural sprays has resulted in a proliferation of flora along these old railway tracks.

Before continuing my journey along this path to Sudbury, I crossed to the Essex side of the river by the Rod Bridge and ascended the hill to Borley church, which has some remarkable neatly clipped yews, with frills and huge round bases, in its churchyard and a commanding view across the Stour valley towards Melford and Lavenham. At the time of the Dissolution of the Monasteries, Henry VIII gave the Borley estate to Edward Waldegrave, an ardent Catholic who was imprisoned twice in the Tower of London. The first occasion was in 1551, during the reign of Edward VI, when he refused to inform the Princess Mary that she should not say Mass in her room, and the second during the reign of Elizabeth I, because he would not take the Oath of Supremacy and ignored the Act of Uniformity. He died in the Tower in 1561 at the age of forty-four and was later interred at Borley church in a massive tomb which dominates the nave.

As I entered the church an irreverent, piping, Cockney voice shouted at me across the nave, "Ah, mister, there is a ghost in 'ere, ain't there?" Not wanting to disappoint the lad, and being aware of the reputation that Borley has for ghosts, I readily agreed and was immediately surrounded by a group of excited youngsters who had come intent on finding a ghost. It was then that I was confronted by a very irate man who was in charge of the boys, who proceeded to inform me that such things did not exist and would I kindly not fill his boys' heads with such stuff and nonsense. Ghosts are a very emotive subject. People, it seems, passionately believe or disbelieve, but are never indifferent to them.

It is not so much Borley Church which has a reputation for being haunted, although the heavy lead coffins in the crypt were alleged at one time to have been mysteriously moved, the wicks from the sanctuary lamp inexplicably removed and, as I write in 1980, there is a letter in the *East Anglian Daily Times* reporting mysterious noises coming from within the church. That reputation is much more attached to the Rectory, which stood on the opposite side of the road until it burnt down in 1939 and was finally demolished in 1944. It had the reputation, probably without justification, of being the most haunted house in England.

Whether the haunting of Borley Rectory is fact, fiction or fancy, it is a remarkable story which caught the imagination of people throughout the

Brundon Mill, one of the many watermills which once took their power from the Stour.

world when it was widely publicised between 1929 and 1939. It still remains a centre of controversy and investigation.

The story of the nun who haunted the rectory began some time during the thirteenth century when, according to legend, a monastery stood on the site of the demolished rectory and was linked by a subterranean passage to a nunnery at Bures, seven miles downstream from Borley. Inevitably a young novice nun fell in love with one of the Brothers from Borley, and they had their clandestine meetings in the woods at Borley. Eventually they eloped in a black coach drawn by two bay horses driven by another Brother from the monastery, but they were chased and caught. The suitor was hanged, or possibly beheaded, and the young nun, as was the custom, bricked up in a Convent wall with the traditional loaf of bread and pitcher of water. It is a pity to spoil this romantic story by recalling that coaches were not built until the middle of the sixteenth century. It is, too, unlikely that nuns were ever punished in the way described, and further there is no evidence of a monastery ever having stood at Borley. Nevertheless, four hundred years later it was the apparition of a nun walking the rectory garden and the phantom coach and horses driven by headless coachmen which was seen and heard clattering and rumbling up Borley hill.

The rectory, an ugly, rambling, red-brick Victorian building, was built in 1862 by the Rector, Henry Bull. By all accounts it was an uncharitable place, cold and cheerless and without facilities such as running water but large enough to accommodate the Rector's fourteen children and his servants. His son, also Henry but known as Harry to avoid confusion, first became the Curate and then succeeded his father in 1892 and remained the Rector until his death in 1927. It was during the period of sixty-five years of the Bull incumbencies that the nun was seen by the Bull family. What happened during the previous four hundred years is not recorded. The apparition had appeared to Mr Bull's sisters at a bedroom window, and downstairs another window was bricked up to prevent the nun staring at them from the garden while they were having their meals.

Ernest Ambrose was organist at Borley for seventeen years. He was appointed in 1896, when he was eighteen years old, and recalls in his book, *Melford Memories*, being told of the phantoms by the Misses Bull, whom he knew well. He described them as being "down to earth women not given to exaggeration or emotionalism," and says they spoke of the phenomena in a matter-of-fact manner.

However he states that although he often left the church late at night after choir practice to walk back to his home at Melford, at no time during his seventeen years as organist did he ever witness any untoward event. Other people have reported hearing the choir and the organ playing long after the organist had locked up and gone home.

The phantom nun has manifested itself to other people beside the Bull family, most notably in 1927 to Fred Cartwright, a journeyman carpenter, who saw the nun standing by the rectory gate on no fewer than four occasions in a fortnight. The last time he saw her, he thought she looked ill and went back to see if he could be of assistance, but she vanished. This story is given little credence by Dingwall in his analysis of the events at Borley in his book, *The Haunting of Borley Rectory*.

It is not certain what prompted the Rev Eric Smith to write to the *Daily Mirror* soon after his appointment to the living at Borley, but by doing so he activated a chain of events which was to make Borley a household name and to give the Rectory the title of "the Most Haunted House in England." According to Dingwall although Smith did not believe in ghosts he was anxious to contact a psychical research society who would allay the fears of his parishioners about the haunted rectory so that they would not be afraid to visit him.

If this was the Rector's intention, his action had precisely the reverse effect. The newspaper contacted Harry Price, a prolific ghost story writer and

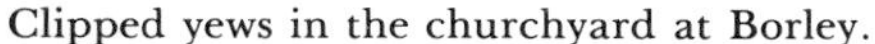
Clipped yews in the churchyard at Borley.

founder member and director of The National Laboratory of Psychical Research. He first visited the Rectory on the 12th June, 1929, and from then on there was increased psychical activity there, with the emergence of new phenomena; stone throwing, tapping of messages on mirrors; voices whispering in the dark "Don't Carlos, don't"; mysterious ringing of the bells used to summon the servants; even a tablet of soap decided to jump out of its dish.

A year later the Smiths decided to move from the Rectory to Long Melford, not because they were worried about the alleged phenomena, which they did not accept as paranormal, but because of the inhospitality of the house and the nuisance caused by the publicity and the visitors who came by the bus load to see the ghost.

In October, 1930, the Rev Lionel Foyster was appointed to the living and during the five years of his incumbency all hell was let loose at the Rectory. According to Harry Price, over 2,000 paranormal phenomena occurred, in the period between October, 1930, and January, 1932. As well as those already mentioned, writing appeared on the inside walls, the grave it seems is no defence against vandalism. There was much missile activity, including bottles, stones and a hammer thrown allegedly by poltergeists; there were outbreaks of fire; and wine, beautiful ruby Chambertin, was turned into jet-black ink, with Sauterne being transformed into eau de Cologne.

It has been alleged that Mrs Foyster, the Rector's wife, was the source of many of the phenomena. In an attempt to pursuade her husband to move from Borley she created or improved on the paranormal to convince him that Borley was not a suitable place for her to live.

"If it is reasonable to suppose that Mrs Foyster wished to leave Borley, whilst her husband was convinced it was his duty to remain, then it may be thought that there was a motive for her to create a superstructure of objective and uncomfortable incidents on the basis of the traditional legend of the rectory, in an endeavour to demonstrate to her husband that life for her in 'the most haunted house in England' was intolerable . . ." The Foysters left Borley in October, 1935.

Several attempts by means of seances and the use of a planchette have been made to communicate with the ghosts. At one seance in London the apparition named herself as Mary Lairre, a French girl who was murdered by strangling in 1667.

Another theory about the identity of the phantom nun is given by a Mrs Dawson, from Colchester, who after considerable research was of the opinion that the nun could have been Arabella Waldegrave, a grandchild of King James II. When he fled to France during the contest for the Protestant succession, the Waldegraves, including Arabella, being ardent Catholics went with him. Arabella was sent to a Convent school at Pontoise and later went to a Convent in Paris to become a nun. This is the last that was heard of the lady, although as Mrs Dawson points out, all the other members of the Waldegrave family have been carefully documented. It is thought that Arabella may have become a spy and found her way back to Borley, where she was murdered.

In another planchette message the researchers were given a premonition that the rectory would be burnt down and that human remains would be found beneath it. The rectory did burn down, on the night of 27th February, 1939, the fire being started when the owner, Captain Gregson, knocked over an oil lamp on to a pile of books he was sorting out in the main hall. Later human remains were found by Harry Price beneath the cellar floor and these were laid to rest in Liston churchard on 29th May, 1945.

Harry Price has written two books about Borley, *The Most Haunted House in England* and *The End of Borley Rectory*. The evidence in both these books came under close scrutiny by Dr E. J. Dingwall, together with Mrs K. M. Goldney and Mr Trevor Hall, when the Council of the Society for Psychical

Borley mill, with its exposed waterwheel.

Research invited them to examine all the Borley evidence. The results of their findings are published in their book *The Haunting of Borley Rectory* in which they attempt to discredit most if not all the evidence presented by Harry Price.

Still the controversy continues, however. In 1979 the President of the British Occult Society, Mr David Farrant, was reported in the *East Anglian Daily Times* as having said that the district round Sudbury appeared to be one of the most haunted areas in Britain, but the society had its own theories on this which he was not prepared to reveal. "We investigated the whole area round Borley," he said. "It seems to us that the phenomenon is not just in the Rectory and the church. Similar sightings, such as unexplainable drops in temperature, sightings of a nun and lights hovering over the ground, have been made in Liston and Cavendish."

I left Borley to return to the river, leaving behind one small group of boys with their noses pressed hard against a barn door as they peered into the gloom, searching anxiously for their ghost, while a lady stood in the middle of the road remonstrating with another group for their belief in the supernatural. Hers was a lost cause.

A couple of braying donkeys announced my arrival back at the river by Borley mill, from where I took the path along the old railway track to walk the two miles to Sudbury.

The Belchamp Brook passes under the railway embankment to struggle between reeds and rushes to reach the Stour. The Belchamps, a name which comes from a Norman derivation of the Anglo-Saxon word meaning a timber-framed homestead, are three of the smallest and most picturesque villages in North Essex. They mark the easterly course of this tiny tributary of the Stour.

The stream rises near the *Cherry Tree Inn* at Belchamp St Paul; a prim little village with white-washed thatched cottages surrounding a green which has its inn, *The Half Moon*, thatched and with typical Essex weatherboard walls proudly displaying the date of its construction, 1685. The church and the manorial hall, St Paul's, stand outside the village and a mile to the north of it, a possible sign that the plague struck here. The Hall, at the time of Shakespeare, was the home of Arthur Golding, whose translations of the Classics were used by Shakespeare to research his own literary works. Golding brought up his nephew, Edward de Vere, 17th Earl of Oxford, at the Hall. Edward also became famous for his poetry during Shakespeare's time and some attribute Shakespeare's work to him.

Separating the church from the Hall is a beautiful lawn surrounded in summer by a glorious display of flowers. The adjacent barn is reputed to have at least one of its timbers a thousand years old, hewn at the time when Athelstan, the first king of England, gave the village to St Paul's cathedral, from which it acquired its name.

Belchamp Otten, the second of the three villages, has a most interesting Norman church complete with box pews and a quaint gallery.

Sturdy cottages with flint-knapped walls stand around the village pond at Belchamp Walter creating, some say, the prettiest of the three Belchamps. Here the Normans after the Conquest planted their vineyards, a process which is now being repeated at several places along the Stour valley. From its quiet, secluded and wooded position the thirteenth-century church, which lies to the east of the village, looks across the Belchamp valley to Bulmer church on the opposite hillside.

The focal point of Belchamp Walter church is the beautifully painted quadrangular pulpit depicting the four evangelists. On the interior north wall, above the ornate entrance to what was believed to have been a chantry, have been uncovered some faint fourteenth-century mural paintings done in red ochre. Most fascinating and crude in contrast to the art work is the wooden candlestick holder dated 1673, once used by the church's bellringers.

I took the path from the old railway cutting which leads back to the Stour at Brundon mill, leaving the railway footpath to encircle Sudbury until it reaches the station south of the town, from where trains still operate to Marks Tey where they join the London to Norwich main line. Brundon mill is a popular place for a picnic and some fishing during the summer months.

From here the river meanders across wide open meadows bearing the names of Little Fulling Pit and Greater Fulling Pit meadows, a reminder of the medieval wool trade along the valley. It then divides, one part touching the town tangentially at the Croft, a delightful open expanse of green bordering the river, the main stream circumnavigating the town on its journey south. Beside the Stour at the Croft a children's paddling pool has been constructed, surrounded by pleasant gardens in memory of a Sudbury family, Roger and Margaret Green and their children Simon and Ian, who were killed in an air disaster in Yugoslavia in 1971.

The Stour now becomes the millstream to Sudbury mill, which has been converted into a hotel. The mill wheel has been carefully preserved and is the principal feature of the hotel's restaurant. A mummified cat was discovered beneath the timber-framed part of the old building during the conversion to a hotel which took place in 1971. It was an old East Anglian custom to bury a live cat beneath a building under construction to protect it from harm by witches, warlocks and fire. After the cat had been disturbed a series of mishaps occurred at the hotel culminating in it being almost burnt to the ground. The management then succumbed to superstition and re-interred the remains of the cat under the foyer of the hotel. Its grave is outlined in brass on the floor. As far as I know, nothing ill has befallen the hotel since.

CHAPTER FIVE

Sudbury to Higham and the Cambridge Brook

SUDBURY is the main town on the Stour, and it must come close to being regarded as the perfect English market town. Its focal point is Market Hill, crowned by St Peter's Church, now unfortunately closed for regular worship but still used for social occasions and exhibitions. Running down the hill on both sides of the market place, its historic streets fan out towards the river, which almost encompasses the town and prevents it from spilling over into Essex.

A weekly market has existed in Sudbury since Domesday. Market days are now Thursday and Saturday, the cattle auction being held in Burkitt's Lane on Thursday mornings. The market was originally held at the bottom of Market Hill at the junction of School Lane and Stour Street. In the fourteenth century it moved to the site in front of the Town Hall at the top of the hill before moving in 1840 to its present position in front of the church, where once stood a row of houses and the old Moot Hall, demolished in 1830. It was in Sudbury Market Place that the last rebels of the Peasants' Revolt were caught and slain in 1381. A large number of headless skeletons were dug out from the Croft and these are thought to have been those of the rebels.

Three annual fairs were held at Sudbury from medieval days to the nineteenth century, two of them, St Bartholomew's and St Gregory's, on Market Hill while St Peter's Day fair was held on the Croft. It is known that Henry Tooley, a sixteenth-century Ipswich merchant, sold fish brought back from Icelandic waters by his ship the *Mary Walsingham* to London merchants at the Croft fair at Sudbury. Gradually shops took precedence, the fairs became merely places for fun, and in Sudbury they were closed down altogether in 1861 as they had become a "hindrance to trade."

At the bottom of Market Hill is the *Anchor*, formerly the *White Hart Inn*, standing at the entrance to Friars Street. It was here that the unfortunate Dr Rowland Taylor stayed on his way from London to Hadleigh, where he was burnt at the stake for his religious beliefs. This was also the inn where the citizens of Sudbury would have enjoyed performances of Shakespeare's plays, which took place in the old inn yard and were acted by the Earl of Leicester's travelling players. As William was a member of this company, it is very likely that he stayed and acted in his own plays at the *White Hart*.

Sudbury took its name from the Saxon settlement known as Suthburh, meaning the fortified town in the south, referring to East Anglia, where the only other place of any size was Norwich in the north. The Saxon settlement was close to the river by the mill and protected by a moat which followed roughly the line of Friars Street and Burkitt's Lane, rejoining the Stour at the Croft.

Sudbury is first mentioned as a town in the *Anglo-Saxon Chronicle* as the place where Alfwin, the Bishop of Dunwich, died in 797 A.D. A royal mint stood on the site of the present municipal offices at Belle Vue House during the time of the Saxon king Ethelred II (979-1016 A.D.), producing coins bearing the names Sudby, Suthby and Sulby. Sudbury was probably one of Boudica's

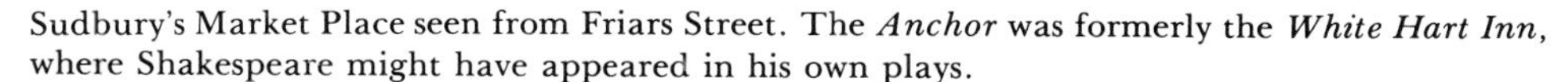
Sudbury's Market Place seen from Friars Street. The *Anchor* was formerly the *White Hart Inn*, where Shakespeare might have appeared in his own plays.

Iceni settlements at the time of the Roman occupation, and before that there is evidence of Bronze Age man dug from the railway cutting at Brundon and also found in the gravel pits there.

At the Conquest Sudbury was Crown property and in due course passed to Robert, Earl of Gloucester, the natural son of Henry I and grandson of the Conqueror. In turn his granddaughter Amicia succeeded to the lordship of Sudbury. She married Richard of Clare, third Earl of Hertford and guardian of the Magna Carta, who died in 1217. The Sudbury estates along with those of Gloucester and Clare passed to their son Gilbert. Sudbury remained the property of the Lords of Clare until the Duke of York, a descendant of the Clare family, became Edward IV (1461) and Sudbury once again became Crown property. Edward VI granted the town to his tutor, Sir John Cheke, in 1551. Two years later when the king died Sir John had to surrender it to Queen Mary, and it was annexed to the Royal Duchy of Lancaster in 1558.

Simon Thebaud of Sudbury was born in 1317 of wealthy parents. His father, a merchant and clothier, provided Elizabeth de Burgh at Clare castle with clothing and furs. Simon, after studying at the universities of Cambridge

The interior of St Gregory's church at Sudbury, with its impressive font cover. Made about 1450, this is similar to the one at Ufford, near Woodbridge.

and Paris, became chaplain to the Pope, who appointed him to the Bishopric of London in 1361 and then promoted him to be the Archbishop of Canterbury in 1375.

Five years later as the Chancellor of England he imposed the Poll tax of 1380, a tax imposed on people to help finance the French war which precipitated Wat Tyler's rebellion. Although Simon took refuge in the Tower of London with his king, Richard II, he was dragged from it by the mob and beheaded on Tower Hill. His head was fixed to a pike and paraded round the streets before being displayed on London Bridge, where it was replaced six days later by that of Wat Tyler.

The Chancellor's body was buried at Canterbury Cathedral but his head was brought back to his home town of Sudbury, where it has since been in the safe keeping of St Gregory's Church on the Croft. Honest Tom Martin of Palgrave recorded in 1727 that an unscrupulous but business-like sexton was in the habit of inserting old teeth into the jaw and selling them as the Archbishop's own teeth to unsuspecting pilgrims seeking holy relics. In 1833 when Simon's tomb at Canterbury was accidentally opened during repairs a lead ball was found inside in place of his head.

St Gregory's Church on the Croft is the mother church of Sudbury. It was probably built on the site of an earlier wooden one. Simon of Sudbury converted it into a collegiate church about 1375 when he built a college near the river on the site of his parents' home, on which now stands Walnut Tree Hospital. The restored brick college gateway is opposite the west end of the church and above it are the arms of Bishop Simon, a Talbot. These dogs, now extinct, were broad-mouthed large-eared hounds, usually white. Simon's motif is now incorporated in Sudbury's coat of arms.

St Gregory's Church is very beautiful inside and particularly impressive is the very tall, ornately carved font cover made about 1450. It is one of the finest examples of a medieval font cover in the country. All Saints' Church at Ballingdon Bridge is the other Sudbury parish church. Its early fourteenth century chancel is the oldest surviving building in Sudbury and it has a very beautifully carved oak pulpit.

From the year 1559 Sudbury had the right to return two Members to Parliament, a privilege not always appreciated as it was accompanied by the obligation of finding two shillings (10p) a day for each M.P. while the House was sitting. The Freemen of Sudbury held the franchise but, as they also constituted the Corporation, it was this body which effectively elected the Members of Parliament; a privilege they claimed as their right in 1702. Sudbury was a typical Rotten Borough in which bribery and corruption at elections was normal practice. A General Election provided a profitable source of income for the electors. As there was no secret ballot they were able to sell their votes, and the owners of the Rotten Boroughs were able to sell the vacant

Parliamentary Seats to aspiring candidates. Once elected, Members of Parliament could trade their parliamentary votes for honours and privileged positions. Candidates would bribe the mob as well as the electors to create riots in which electors could be intimidated into voting for a favoured candidate.

At Sudbury unsuccessful candidates petitioned against the election result as a matter of course, but when in 1841 the petition succeeded the complainants were unable to accept the Seat as they were also guilty of corruption. Over four thousand pounds was paid out in bribes during this election. The landlord of the *Black Boy* on Market Hill showed me a small glass window in the lounge bar through which the bribes, two gold sovereigns, were passed to corrupt electors, who, after voting, went to the *Swan* for a further four gold sovereigns, again paid through a small window so that the person paying out the money would not be seen.

In 1826 Plum Pudding Wilkes offered more modest bribes. He was so named because he provided the electors and their families with dinner on election day. At the by-election of 1834 when both candidates polled 263 votes, the Mayor gave his casting vote in favour of the Tory candidate. There

was an appeal and a new election held on 6th January, 1835. Dickens, who was then a newspaper reporter, had come to Sudbury to report the election for his paper. He later described in *Pickwick Papers* similar goings-on at Eatanswill in the election contest between the Hon. Samuel Slumkey, Tory, and the Hon. Horatio Fizkin, Whig.

"Fizkin's people have got three-and-thirty voters in the lock-up coach-house at the White Hart." This could only be the *Anchor*, formerly the *White Hart*, at the bottom of Market Hill.

"They keep 'em locked up there, till they want 'em," resumed the little man. "The effect of that is, you see, to prevent our getting at them; and even if we could, it would be of no use, for they keep them very drunk for the purpose."

Neither party was beyond putting laudanum, tincture of opium, in their opponents' drinks to send them to sleep until after the poll or to bribe a coachman to overturn his coach, throwing the voters into the river.

In 1907 the inauguration of the Eatanswill Club took place at Sudbury not, I hasten to add, to perpetrate the misdeeds of their forebears but to

Opposite: The Eatanswill Pickwick Club on their way through the Stour valley by stage coach.

Right: A Dickensian picnic beside the Stour. The Eatanswill Pickwick Club is very active raising money for charity.

associate themselves with the fine works of Charles Dickens. After a lapse of several years the Eatanswill Pickwick Club was reconstituted on 28th January, 1973, with Mr Wardle as chairman and headquarters at the Ballingdon Bridge Hotel, where the Eatanswill motto, "Temperance Above All Things," is emblazoned over the bar.

The Hon. Samuel Slumkey and the Hon. Horatio Fizkin still do battle at the Sudbury hustings and publish the most outrageous accusations in the completely biassed *Eatanswill Gazette*, all in aid of local charities. The Whig paper, the *Eatanswill Independent*, seems to have been suppressed. In the latest copy of the *Eatanswill Gazette* I read that Fizkin, when elected, intends to increase the declining population of the town and, if that was not enough, intends to capture the monster out of the Stour, which his opponent Slumkey insists he has removed to Loch Ness!

Because of the corrupt election of 1841, the special parliamentary commission recommended that Sudbury be disfranchised. This was on the 29th July, 1844, when Sudbury became part of the county constituency. In 1950 Sudbury became part of the new Sudbury and Woodbridge constituency.

The old navigation basin at the bottom of Quay Lane, off Friars Street, was the terminus for the horse-drawn barges which came up the river with coal and took away Sudbury bricks for the construction of such prominent London

Opposite: Throwing bricks by hand at Bulmer brickworks.

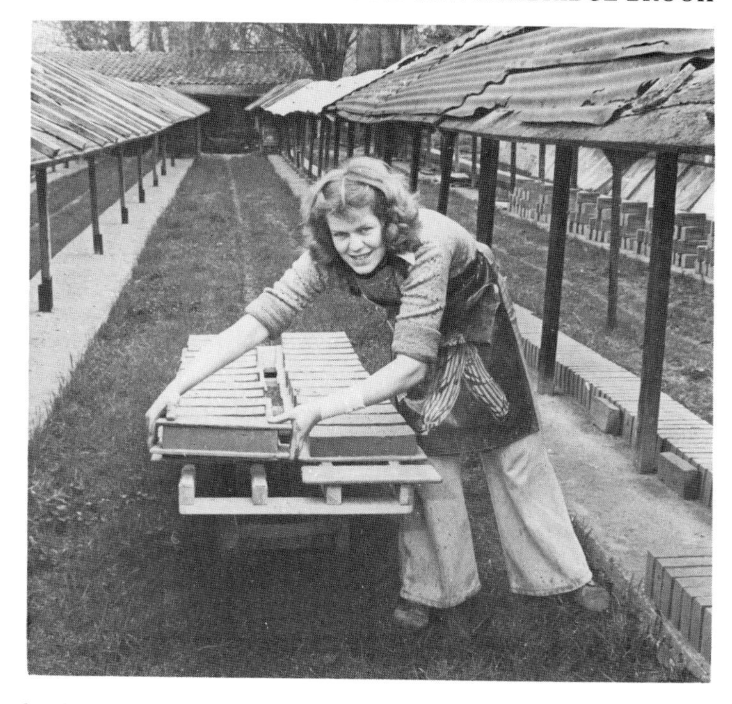

Right: Stacking green bricks in the hacks to dry.

buildings as the Royal Albert Hall and South Kensington museums. The old quay has recently been restored by the River Stour Trust using bricks taken from the demolished Mistley maltings, which had been built with bricks, Ballingdon Reds, from Sudbury.

Although brickmaking at Sudbury has now ceased, it reached its zenith just before the first world war, a cataclysm from the effects of which it never recovered.

I did stumble across one small brickyard on the outskits of Sudbury, The Bulmer Brick and Tile Company, which is still making hand-moulded bricks in much the same way as they were made in Tudor times. The Flemings, as well as giving a new impetus to the art of weaving in East Anglia, re-introduced the technique of brickmaking, lost since Roman times.

As Peter Minter showed me round his brickyard, he explained that the London clay on his site, one of several such outcrops along the Stour valley, had probably been used by Bronze Age man. There was evidence to suggest Roman and Anglo-Saxon occupation of his land, and the remains of a medieval brick kiln had been found. The rustic, higgledy-piggledy array of old red-brick kilns and buildings, some possessing twisted Tudor chimneys, with trailing plants adorning the cottages now used as offices, gave the place an old-world atmosphere which was more akin to a farm than a factory.

It is in fact both a farm and a factory. From early times bricks were produced on farms, the labourers working in the fields during the summer, in the maltings in the autumn and in the brickyard during the winter months. Peter is no exception, as he makes bricks all the year round and farms the adjoining 150 acres of land.

The present records of the Bulmer works go back to 1843. Its maximum output was in 1914 and it was still producing three million bricks a year up to 1939, while watching twenty or thirty brickyards closing around it. Peter's father bought the brickyard in 1936 when he began to restore old cottages, thus creating his own demand for new "old bricks". The present trend in the conservation and restoration of the fabric of our English heritage has resulted in an increasing demand for individually made bricks of various shapes and sizes to replace those which have weathered and crumbled.

The clay is dug from the seam a year before it is used and spread out in a heap on the ground to weather. Having been wetted, it is worked over with a fork known as a crome before being kneaded into the correct consistency by a mechanical pug-mill, which contains an Archimedean screw. This is the only concession to modernisation. In early times horses were used to pug the clay, either by treading it or by providing the power to rotate blades fitted to a central shaft which worked the clay in a vertical barrel. It was also worked by human feet.

I watched a young and pretty lady, Caroline Willingham, take the pugged clay, roll it into a warp, a sausage shape the approximate size of the mould, and then throw it into a sanded, wooden, mould. The sand prevents the clay from sticking to the mould and helps to give the brick texture and enhance its colour. After smoothing off the top of the bricks, she took them outside on a cradle barrow and stacked them with plenty of air space around them in a hack, a shed with a top but no sides. They are now known as green bricks and are left to dry before being fired in a dome-shaped kiln.

Today's modern industry in Sudbury consists of light engineering, which produces components for the motor trade, and the weaving of silk, which has its roots way back in the woollen industry of the fourteenth century when King Edward III encouraged the Flemish weavers to settle in the town. Although the immigrants gave an impetus to the cloth industry they did not modify the type of cloth already produced, kersey, from Kersey and linsey, from Lindsey, both rough homespun cloths. The importance of Sudbury at this period was not so much as a manufacturer of cloth, Hadleigh being the main woollen producing town, but as a collecting centre and market town to which woollens came from weavers throughout the Stour valley to be distributed to the London mercers. As the "Old Draperies" declined towards the end of the sixteenth century, Dutch immigrants came to the town and introduced the manufacture of a new, lighter and finer cloth. Sudbury became the Suffolk centre for these

"New Draperies", and was noted for its Bays, a light twilled worsted, and Says, a fine serge, and its bunting. However the importation of new materials, namely cotton and silk, soon brought the "New Draperies" into decline.

Defoe wrote of Sudbury in 1722, "the number of poor is almost ready to eat up the rich," but Sudbury was to be lucky. The silk industry, which had been started at Spitalfields on what was then the outskirts of London by Huguenots, who had come to England to escape from persecution in France, expanded into the country towns when the wages of the silk weavers were made prohibitively high by the Spitalfields Act of 1774. Cheap skilled labour was found in the declining wool towns of East Anglia.

Two London firms, Vanners Silks and Stephen Walters, the oldest existing silk weaving firm in the country (they made the silk lining for the Coronation Robe of Queen Elizabeth II) came to Sudbury, while the Gainsborough Silk Weaving Company, which now has its factory on the new industrial estate at Chilton, was begun in Sudbury by Reginald Warner in 1903 when he started weaving quality silk fabrics in his cottage. Gainsborough silk has been used to curtain the Houses of Parliament, Clarence House, St James's Palace, the Norwegian Royal Palace in Oslo and British Embassies throughout the world. Their trade mark, a silhouette of Gainsborough, was copied from the house sign which hung outside the artist's birthplace when it was used as tea-rooms. The company purchased the sign but have now returned it to the Gainsborough House Society, who have replaced it above the doorway of Gainsborough's old home.

Thomas Gainsborough, the best known and most admired of English portrait painters, is the pride of Sudbury as his monument by Sir Bertram MacKennal placed at the focal point of the town on Market Hill testifies. It was unveiled as a national memorial to the artist on 10th June, 1913, by Princess Louise, the daughter of King Edward VII. Thomas was born in a house in Sepulchre Street, now re-named after the artist, although he is quoted as saying to a friend, W. H. Pyne, that he was born in a mill: "Old pimply-nosed Rembrandt and myself were both born in a mill."* His birth date is unknown, but he was baptized at the Independent Meeting Room on 14th May, 1727.

Gainsborough's birthplace, now open to the public, dates back to the Tudor period, when it was two houses, one of them later being used as the *Black Horse Inn*, but only two rooms from this time survive in the present building. A nineteenth century engraving by George Finden shows the topsy-turvy Tudor houses with their overhanging jetties and the typically Suffolk ornate pargetting round the windows. In marked contrast the present dignified but dull Georgian front was added by the artist's father when he modernised the premises in 1723 for use as a workshop as well as being his home.

*W. T. Whitley. *Thomas Gainsborough,* page 2.

Gainsborough's birthplace at Sudbury, with the cut-out sign which became the trade mark of a local silk-weaving firm.

Gainsborough's father was a wealthy clothier who introduced the technique of making woollen shrouds to Sudbury. He married Mary Burrough, the sister of the Rev Humphrey Burrough, Headmaster of Sudbury Grammar School, and they had nine children. The artist's second brother Humphrey is believed to have invented a steam engine, though this invention has been attributed to James Watt. Thomas, the artist, was the fifth son to be born into the family and while still at school he commenced the picture *Wood Scene, Village of Cornard* which so impressed his father that he sent him to London at the age of thirteen to learn his craft.

Thomas was only nineteen when he married Margaret Burr, said to have been the illegitimate daughter of the Duke of Beaufort, but happily for the artist she was financially well endowed. The couple returned to Sudbury and took a house in Friars Street, where their first daughter Mary was born. Two of Gainsborough's major works were completed while he was at Sudbury; the painting *Mr and Mrs Robert Andrews*, the squire and his wife who lived on Ballingdon hill, was painted against a background of the surrounding countryside, and the landscape *Cornard Wood.* Although Gainsborough gained prominence as a portrait artist, landscape painting gave him the most pleasure but "landskip" was more difficult to sell than portraits.

John Constable wrote later of Gainsborough, "I fancy I see Gainsborough in every hedge and hollow tree."

It would be nice to think that Gainsborough found his initial inspiration, first expressed in his *Wood Scene, Village of Cornard,* in the beauty of the Stour valley. Later the artist left Sudbury for Ipswich, from where he went to Bath before taking up residence in London, where he died from cancer at the age of sixty-one. He was buried in the little churchyard at Kew.

Gainsborough Street passes into Stour Street, which leads back to the river. It contains two splendid half-timbered Tudor houses, the Chantry and Salters Hall, now a private school, decorated with the beautiful ornate wood carving of the period.

The present Ballingdon Bridge, a concrete structure, is the fifth bridge to carry the road across the Stour at this point, which was on the main pilgrim route from London to St Edmund's shrine at Bury. Many sovereigns have

Thomas Gainsborough looks down on bargain-hunters at Sudbury Market. But the paintings are not Gainsborough's.

passed this way to pay homage to the saint, both King John and Edward III staying in Sudbury en route to Bury.

On the north side of the bridge, on the site now occupied by the Ballingdon Bridge Hotel, stood in the thirteenth century St John's hospital belonging to the Knights Templar, the guardians of pilgrims, which was maintained with the tolls from the bridge.

Beyond the hotel the river flows through ancient water meadows, which together form the Common Land of Sudbury. These meadows have belonged to the burgesses and freemen of Sudbury since the middle of the thirteenth century, when Richard de Clare granted in the year 1260 the pastures of Portmanscroft (now the Freemen's Great Common and the Freemen's Little Common) and the Kingsmarsh to the burgesses of Sudbury. The present freemen of Sudbury, who have inherited their titles, are very proud of this charter which measures only nine inches by three and a half inches.

The extent of the Common Land has been increased by the addition of the Fullingpit meadow and the North meadow. This land is of considerable scientific interest as the meadows have the longest continuous grazing record of any in East Anglia. Today the grazing and fishing rights are vested in the Trustees of the Common Land of Sudbury, who administer these rights on behalf of the freemen, and through the trust the residents of Sudbury enjoy free fishing rights along this part of the river

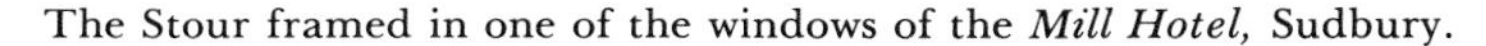

The Stour framed in one of the windows of the *Mill Hotel,* Sudbury.

The Stour now passes under Ballingdon Bridge to skirt the town flowing through the beautiful Friars meadows before turning south to leave the town near Great Cornard Church with its tall, elegant, shingled spire.

From Sudbury the Stour meanders south through a flat flood plain to reach the *White Swan* at Henny Street on the Essex side of the river. It was on a field opposite the *Swan*, Sharpfight Meadow, that Boudica caught up with and slaughtered a Roman Legion. This might possibly have been the Ninth Legion whose burial ground has been found at Wormingford, further down the river.

Henny also has the legend of two dragons, one black and the other red with spots, who fought each other across the river. When red won both victor and vanquished retired back into the hills. This could have been a colourful fifteenth-century description of the fighting which took place hereabouts between the Saxons and the Danes. The *Swan* was a popular drinking place for the old bargemen and is now a Mecca for thirsty weekend anglers who fish the river.

Daws Hall stands in sixty acres of beautiful parkland above the river where a small tributary enters the Stour near Pitmire lock. Inside, the Hall displays its Tudor oak beams, whilst outside its age is disguised by an attractive Georgian front. The owner, Major Iain Grahame, told me that he has heard the footsteps of a phantom dog padding round the house and has seen the apparition of a woman staring at him from an upstairs window. This is possibly that of a woman killed in the house by a burglar. Once every year a smell of burning pervades the house on the anniversary of the day that it once caught fire.

It is, however, birds and not ghosts that interest the major, whose aim is to breed those wildfowl and pheasants from all parts of the world which are threatened with extinction. At present nineteen of the forty-eight species of pheasant in danger are on his wildfowl farm in the grounds of Daws Hall. Iain Grahame with his wife Didy and the help of friends has founded the World Pheasant Association, with its headquarters at Daws Hall, in the hope of preserving these beautiful birds for future generations.

He explained to me that "It is not simply a matter of taking birds from captivity back to their natural environment and releasing them. The natural habitat must be first surveyed to find the most suitable area which can be controlled by making it into a nature reserve. The co-operation of the local people must be sought, and the birds while they are in captivity must be fed on food they will find in the wild as they are released. A reintroduction programme in Pakistan, based on these principles, is proving very successful."

Iain Grahame's greatest success has been the breeding of the Himalayan Blood Pheasant, the rarest birds in his collection. His is one of only three establishments in the world which have succeeded in breeding these birds in

The remains of Pitmire Lock behind Daws Hall, Lamarsh. The beam braced the two uprights and prevented the weight of the gates from moving them out of position.

captivity. As I left a flock of free-winged barnacle geese took off and circled overhead. They preferred life on the farm to that in the wild—who can blame them?

Having passed Pitmire the Stour flows between steep rounded hills, St Edmund's Hill on the Suffolk side and Lamarsh Hill in Essex, from where there are fine panoramic views of the valley and the river as it tumbles over a small weir. The round Norman tower of Lamarsh church tucked into the base of the hill and cloaked in trees gives this remote corner of Essex a delightful, Continental, almost a wonderland, atmosphere. The Norman round tower, one of only three in Essex, was built about 1140 A.D. The interesting conical spire, which adds its own character to the church, was not built until the nineteenth century. The brick porch is Elizabethan.

It is strange to think that the manors of Lamarsh and Henny, here beside the Stour, belonged to the Scottish Crown during the twelfth century when the Earl of Huntingdon, Lord of the Manor of Lamarsh, became King David I of Scotland. The Scots rarely had the opportunity to exercise their rights and in 1237 Henry III considered that the Scottish estates in England were his property and gave Lamarsh with Henny to his Judge, Philip Basset, whose family have been described as the first professional legal family in England.

The little town of Bures, hardly more than a village, where John Constable's grandfather was a farmer, is the only place in the Stour valley where the river goes through the middle of the town dividing it equally between Essex and Suffolk. Consequently it is controlled by no fewer than three district councils and shared between two Parliamentary Constituencies, Sudbury and Woodbridge and Saffron Walden. Bures St Mary on the Suffolk side of the river is controlled by Babergh District Council, Bures Hamlet across the river by Braintree District Council and Mount Bures is controlled by Colchester Borough Council.

The town is grouped round its fourteenth-century church, on the Suffolk side of the bridge linking the two counties. The original church of Bures was in existence before Domesday and belonged to the Abbey at Caen in Normandy. Construction of the tower, the oldest part of the present building, was financed by Sir Richard Waldegrave, Lord of the Manor, M.P. and Speaker of the House, before he died in 1410. The spire which surmounted the tower was burnt down in 1733 when it was struck by lightning, the heat from the blaze being sufficient to melt the bells inside.

Beyond the town, in the midst of beautiful, rolling Suffolk countryside, stands a small thatched chapel on the top of a remote hillside. It was built in the thirteenth century as the private chapel of Gilbert de Tany, Lord of the Manor, and consecrated by the Archbishop of Canterbury, Stephen Langton, in 1218. The church became neglected at the Reformation and was later used as a barn until it was restored in 1920 by a Bures lady, Miss Badcock, whose sister was the model for the drawings of Alice in Wonderland. The chapel now contains the monuments of the de Vere family, which were housed in Earls Colne Priory until it collapsed. Here lies Alberic de Vere, the first Great Chamberlain of England who died in 1141, surrounded by the tombs of the fifth, eighth and eleventh Earls of Oxford.

The chapel was built at the place where Edmund is said to have been crowned King of East Anglia on Christmas Day, 855, in the royal town of Bures. Traditionally Edmund is said to have been born in Saxony, from where he sailed when he was about thirteen years old to claim his English crown. He is thought to have landed near Hunstanton on the Norfolk coast. According to the Augustinian Canon Geoffrey of Wells, writing about 1150, after the assassination of King Ethelbert some members of the House of Uffa moved to Old Saxony. When King Offa, the last of the English branch of the Uffings, found himself without an heir he adopted Edmund from the Saxon branch of the family. Thus Edmund is said to be a descendant of the House of Uffa.

After a short reign of fourteen years, Edmund was killed by the Danish invaders after the battle of Thetford in 869. Abbo of Fleury records that

Left: The round tower of Lamarsh church with its nineteenth-century spire.

Opposite: The interior of the thirteenth-century St Stephen's chapel at Bures with tombs of the de Vere family, Earls of Oxford.

Edmund fled from the battlefield and was captured and killed at a place called Haeglisdun. But where is it? Hoxne, on the Suffolk-Norfolk border, has for long claimed to be the place where the king hid under a bridge until the sunlight glinting off his golden spurs alerted a newly wed couple returning home across the bridge, who then betrayed him to the Danes. Edmund is said to have placed a curse on future newlyweds crossing this bridge, so most couples avoid the bridge. Hellesdon near Norwich has also found favour, but recently another contender has been discovered fifteen miles north of Bures at Bradfield St Clare, close to Bury St Edmunds, where a field name has provided a new clue. I think it logical that the king would have escaped from the battle and fled to the safety of Bures.

Across the valley is the parish of Mount Bures, which takes its name from the Norman mound, now covered with trees and shrubs, standing next to the church. It is a picture in springtime when it is covered with bluebells poking their way through the long grass. Local people refer to it as Boudica's Mount. A grave of a Belgic prince, dated about 43 A.D. was uncovered when the

railway cutting was made in 1849. The church was restored in 1875 when the Sussex broach spire was added. Mount Bures stands above the Cambridge Brook, a small tributary which flows into the Stour near Bures mill.

Reference has already been made to the fighting dragons of Henny, but a dragon was also, so it is said, brought to Bures by a crusader returning from the Holy Land; many went from Bures on the Crusades. It was not a very well-behaved dragon, and after running amok among the villagers it dived into the Stour and swam downstream to the Wormingford decoy, where it took refuge. The decoy today remains a dark and gloomy place. When Bures lake was excavated to provide sand for the construction of Ipswich power station the remains of a prehistoric monster were uncovered. With some imagination this could have been the dragon, but it is referred to in the village as the dinosaur. Colchester museum suggested that it was most likely to have been an elephant. It proved impossible to extricate the remains, apart from a tooth which weighed two and a half pounds.

It was at Bures lake that I first met Len Head, who is recognised

Wissington mill, with its lucam through which sacks were hoisted to the garner floor.

nationwide as an authority on tench fishing and has caught more tench over seven pounds in weight than anybody else in the country. Anglers, it seems, are a tenacious but cheerful breed. Torrential rain had been falling since dawn, when Len had started fishing. It was still falling when I arrived mid-morning. Clutching my tape recorder and camera I perched precariously on the side of a steep slippery slope, getting what shelter I could from one of those brightly coloured canopies which I always thought were to keep off the sun. It is always fascinating to watch an expert at work even under these conditions, and I was very grateful to Len when he later offered to write the notes about angling on the Stour, which I have placed in full in the appendix.

The river flows through the last of its ninety-degree turns before passing Smallbridge Hall, where Queen Elizabeth I stayed on two separate occasions. It cost her host, Sir Richard Waldegrave, £250, which would represent a fortune today.

The Stour now divides before passing round Nayland, the main stream curving behind a row of quaint cottages in Bear Street to enhance their pretty gardens before it tumbles over an elaborate weir to pass under Abell's bridge to join again the other half of the river. The bridge was named after its benefactor, the rich clothier John Abell, who in 1523 left sufficient funds for the maintenance of the bridge. He is commemorated with a stone plaque bearing a bell surmounted by the letter "A" placed on each side of the bridge, which replaced a wooden structure in 1775.

Time like the river has passed Nayland by. The village has not succumbed to twentieth-century commercialism, industrialism or tourism, but boasts instead of its past glory and prosperity as one of Suffolk's fifteenth-century centres of weaving. Its church contains a rare treasure, an original Constable painting of Christ blessing the bread and wine painted on the altar reredos.

Nayland is justly proud of one of its citizens, Dr Jane Walker, who pioneered the open-air treatment of tuberculosis at the beginning of the century and founded the hospital bearing her name in the countryside just outside the town. The disease has been conquered and the hospital is now used for the treatment of handicapped people. I am glad they, too, have the advantage of this delightful countryside.

The Stour now becomes inaccessible as it flows between high hills on which stand Stoke-by-Nayland and Boxted, from where the best views of this

Collecting rushes for basketmaking from the Stour near Nayland.

part of the valley can be appreciated. If anybody thinks that East Anglia is flat they should come here and look across to Suffolk to the majestic tower of Stoke Church dominating the skyline. To the east the tributaries Box and Brett cut deep into the rolling countryside, for ever shaping the landscape as they flow south to join the Stour, which comes into view again to form a picturesque corner at Boxted mill.

It is now but a short distance to where Langham mill once stood. Sir Alfred Munnings wrote of this place, "To use the word arcadia here is not affectation. No other word could describe Langham mill, its lock, bridge, mill-pool, flood-gates and trees."

All have gone now to be replaced by a pumping station which takes water from the Stour at a rate of about 45 million litres a day which, after treatment at the filtration plant beside the river, is pumped to Tiptree and Danbury for distribution to Essex consumers as far south as the Thames. The Essex Water

The Stour at Boxted, Essex.

Company who operate the Langham, Stratford St Mary and Cattawade pumping stations provide one and a third million customers with 340 million litres of water every day. Their Stratford pumping station can lift up to 159 million litres of water a day, which is transferred from the Stour via the Ardleigh reservoir to the Abberton reservoir for storage during the winter months. The recently installed automatic pumps at Cattawade can pump an additional 13.6 million litres per day, which is also stored at Abberton reservoir.

I do not begrudge the waterworks its position or Essex their water, as do many anglers and conservationists. The water is essential and the buildings not unattractive, but I do wish that the little bridge across the river could be restored so that the footpaths linking Langham and Stratford with Higham and Thorington Street could be used again. At this point the River Box, the first of the two main tributaries of the Stour, enters the river and within a mile the second, the River Brett, joins the main river by Higham Church.

CHAPTER SIX

The Box and the Brett

A MULBERRY tree, gnarled and twisted with age, still bears fruit in defiance of the elements as it has done for the last five hundred years on the top of an exposed, windswept plateau above the Box valley. The tree is all that remains of the Groton Manor estate, the home of John Winthrop, and it is symbolic of the fortitude, determination and courage of this devout Puritan who emigrated from this place to found the Colony of Massachusetts and to lay the foundation of the United States of America.

John Winthrop was born in the next village, Edwardstone, on 12th January, 1588, the son of a family of wealthy clothiers who had come from Lavenham. Today Edwardstone is nothing more than a scattered parish of about three hundred people in two thousand acres of agricultural land. Its isolated church is reached by passing under a folly, a brick archway modelled after Temple Bar in London and constructed in 1840.

On an occasion when a horse entered the church during a service to shelter from a thunderstorm, its owner mounted it and galloped down the aisle and out of the church. For this irreverent act, committed in 1637, Edward Alston was given a penance of twenty marks (£13) to be paid to St Paul's Cathedral for its improvement.

John Winthrop entered Trinity College, Cambridge, when he was fourteen, married for the first time when he was seventeen, became a Justice of the Peace at eighteen, holding his first Court in Groton Hall, which still stands next to Groton church, when he was twenty-one. He became a lawyer and was admitted to the Inner Temple in 1628, two years before he sailed in the *Arbella* for America. He was the father of sixteen children from his four marriages.

It was not entirely religious intolerance, political instability, or corrupt practices in the English courts that prompted Winthrop to believe that God's work was better done overseas. His financial situation had been affected by a slump in the wool trade in 1620, which created rising prices and roaring inflation, whilst the rents of his tenants remained fixed by law. For some unknown reason, he also lost his legal practice.*

The first expedition of four vessels arrived at Salem in Massachusetts Bay in June, 1631, but Winthrop not liking the place moved on to Charlestown and then crossed the river Charles to establish the town of Boston. The Trading

**America*, by Alistair Cooke.

Charter which Winthrop took with him had been carefully and subtly drafted by him so that it effectively gave the new colony its independence from England, although they still recognised the authority of the king.

John Winthrop's sister Lucy married Emmanuel Downing and they joined her brother in New England in 1638. Their son George was one of the first students of Harvard University, formerly called Cambridge but renamed after a benefactor, and he had a distinguished, if somewhat chequered, political and diplomatic career. His name is perpetuated in Downing Street, London, where parts of the house he built are incorporated into the present No. 10, the official residence of the Prime Minister. George Downing, the grandson, founded Downing College, Cambridge, with the fortunes left by his grandfather.

From the neighbouring village of Little Waldingfield, which together with the pretty thatched cottages of Great Waldingfield, marks the source of the River Box, Samuel Appleton emigrated with his family to settle on land at Ipswich, named after the Suffolk town, adjacent to that of his friend John Winthrop. The descendants of both families have given loyal and distinguished service to their country. Abraham Lincoln's secretary was an Appleton and Fanny Appleton married the poet Longfellow.

John Winthrop, born in 1936, is the senior of the present family and chairman of Wood, Struthers and Winthrop, members of the New York Stock Exchange. In his grandfather's generation Beekman Winthrop was the first Governor of Puerto Rico and Under-Secretary of the Navy to President Theodore Roosevelt. His first cousin Fred is the Commissioner of Agriculture in Massachusetts.

Groton Hall, where John Winthrop held court as a Justice of the Peace, and Groton church.

There are two places in New England named after Groton on the Box, one in Massachusetts and one in Connecticut. The son of the founder of New England, also John, was appointed the Governor of Connecticut in 1657.

In 1875 the American descendants of John Winthrop installed a stained glass window in the English church of Groton in memory of John Winthrop, "The Father of New England", whilst outside is the tomb of his father Adam and that of his grandfather.

By the time it reaches the little town to which it gave its name, the Box has become a young lively stream enjoying its adolescence as it flows, gurgling over the pebbles, beside the village street. It is incredible to think, looking at the stream now just an inch or two deep that it was once navigable as far as the church; the route by which the Caen stone was brought to build it. This could be a very pretty corner if the telegraph poles were removed and the myriad electric cables and telephone wires concealed. The massive fifteenth-century church shows its age. Its elaborately carved south porch, partly made from a soft sandstone, is badly weathered whilst the north porch—one of the finest examples of fourteenth century decorated woodwork—is in need of restoration. This porch may have been moved to the church from a nearby monastery at an unknown date. In contrast the stained glass east window portraying the Transfiguration of Christ is of modern design. It is in memory of Captain Ralph Vernon and his wife, members of the congregation of Boxford church. The artist Rosemary Rutherford died shortly after completing the work. There is also a memorial in the church to Elizabeth Hyam, who died at the age of a hundred and twelve, having outlived four husbands.

Boxford was prominent amongst the wool towns of the "Old Draperies" whose merchants minted their own currency, brass farthings, which were more acceptable to their customers than the official currency. Hence, presumably, the phrase "not worth a brass farthing". The Huguenots brought with them to Boxford the art of glove-making and also the dressing of deer skins, at one time an important industry in the town.

It was from Boxford that police constable Ayres set out for London to initiate the arrest of William Corder for the murder of Maria Marten in the Red Barn, so called because of the red tint created by the sunlight falling on it, at Polstead, a quiet pretty village overlooking the Box valley two miles south of Boxford.

Maria Marten was born at Polstead in 1801. At the age of seven she was sent to work as a domestic servant to a parson at Layham, but returned home three years later to look after her father and family when their mother died. Her father, a farm labourer and the village mole-catcher, married again when Maria was eighteen. By now she had become a vivacious, attractive and a promiscuous young woman. Her first known affair was with Thomas Corder, who later met an untimely death by drowning when he tried to cross the frozen

Maria Marten's cottage at Polstead.

village pond. By him she had her first child, which died shortly after birth. When Thomas deserted her Maria sought solace in Peter Matthews, with whom she was having an affair whilst courting Corder, and he sired her second child, a healthy boy whom she called Thomas Henry. She received £5 a quarter from the father for the child's maintenance.

Maria now became fatally infatuated with William Corder, Thomas's younger brother, four years her junior, the son of a prosperous farmer. Their child, Maria's third, also died in infancy.

The events which led up to Maria's death in the barn and the manner in which she died on Friday, 18th May, 1827, have never been known with certainty and a mystery still remains. William, it seems, promised after much persuasion to take Maria to Ipswich and marry her and suggested that they meet in the Red Barn. She was to go alone in male attire because, Corder told her, the local policeman had a warrant for her arrest on a charge of bringing illegitimate children into the world.

Maria did as she was told, but never emerged from that barn. She died either by shooting, strangulation, stabbing or a combination of these methods, either at the hands of Corder or someone else, by accident during a struggle, or even by her own hand after being jilted.

If it was murder, the motive was equally mysterious. Possibly Corder found marriage to a social inferior distasteful; it might have been that Maria was blackmailing him into marriage by threatening to expose him as the murderer of her child, in which case they would both be implicated; perhaps Maria threatened to report her lover as the thief who took her money from her. It has also been alleged that Maria's stepmother Anne was infatuated with Corder and was a party to the murder so that she could eliminate her rival.

All that is certain is that Maria died and was buried in the barn. Corder continued to work on the land until after the harvest, when he left Polstead for a holiday in London. He had allegedly told Maria's parents and other enquirers that Maria was lodging in Ipswich awaiting a special licence allowing them to marry, and then wrote from London that they had married and were living in the Isle of Wight, although the letter was post-marked London.

That winter apparently Corder placed a matrimonial advertisement in the *Sunday Times* and the *Morning Herald* to which he received no fewer than ninety-five replies from ladies seeking matrimony, including one from Miss Mary Moore, whom Corder had previously met on two occasions. They married and his wife opened a school for girls at Brentford, where they went to live. It was about this time that Corder is supposed to have presented a false cheque for £93 to a Manningtree bank.

Meanwhile Maria's parents were becoming more anxious about Maria, as she had not written personally to them, and when Mrs Marten had recurring dreams, so she said, that Maria had been murdered in the Red Barn she sent her husband to investigate; he found her body on 19th April, 1828. It has been alleged that Mrs Marten knew of the murder all the time and that she decided to betray Corder when he ceased to send her money.

A London policeman, Constable Lea, arrested Corder and handed him over to Constable Ayres at the *Red Lion* in Brentford. The following day, having said farewell to his pregnant wife, the prisoner was brought under escort by coach to Colchester, where he stayed the night at the *George Hotel*, as the prison governor would not accept responsibility for him, before being brought to the old *Cock Inn*, next door to the present public house, at Polstead. The inquest on Maria was resumed and Corder committed for trial at the next Bury Assizes. Because of conflicting medical evidence, Maria's body was exhumed in the early hours of one morning in Polstead churchyard to try and ascertain the cause of death. William Corder was found guilty of murder and hanged outside Bury gaol on Monday, 11th August, 1828, the last public hanging in Bury St Edmunds.

The nauseating part of this saga is the obnoxious obscenities created by a morbid public. People fought and jostled with each other in an attempt to get into the courtroom. They followed Corder on his journey from Polstead to

The home of William Corder, Maria Marten's lover, who was hanged for her murder.

Bury St Edmunds, where twenty thousand flocked to witness the execution. Corder was left dangling in front of this crowd for an hour before he was taken down and slit up his middle, his innards to be displayed on a trestle table in the Shire Hall, while five thousand filed past him to satisfy their morbid curiosity. The hangman sold the rope at a guinea an inch and later the surgeon George Creed bound a copy of the history of the murder with Corder's skin.

Numerous plays and books were written both during and after the trial and the Murder in the Red Barn became one of the best known and most publicised crimes of the century. Maria Marten was finally laid to rest in Polstead churchyard but her gravestone was desecrated by souvenir hunters, who took pieces away until now there is none of it left. Poor Maria.

Recent research suggests there might well have been a miscarriage of justice and does much to vindicate the accused. Poor Corder!

Polstead, at one time famous for its little black cherries, takes its name, meaning the place of pools, from the numerous ponds it possessed. The story is told that from one of them rose the ghosts of a coach and four horses after they had crashed into the pond, having been bewitched by an old farmer. The apparition of the Rector, who had exorcised these ghosts, later replaced the coach and horses as he rode round the village in a trap drawn by a headless horse.

In 1980 the *East Anglian Daily Times* reported that the then Rector, the Rev Hayden Foster, was having trouble with a ghost at Polstead Rectory. He told a reporter that, "About 3 a.m. we were lying half awake, when Margot", his wife, "saw the walls of the bedroom change from being freshly painted to peeling, damp, old wallpaper—just as it might have looked 20 or 30 years ago. She heard screaming like a child—but it wasn't Gerard—and she felt like she was being suffocated or strangled . . ."

"I felt too, that there was real danger in that room. There's a definite feeling of evil in that place . . ."

The rector and his family moved from the Rectory into a cottage in the village.

Polstead Church, parts of which date from the twelfth century, stands high on a hillside overlooking the steep sides of the V-shaped Box valley cloaked in serene English parkland, through which, until recently, wandered herds of deer. This pretty church in its idyllic setting is unique as it possesses the only stone spire in Suffolk, while inside the church is supported by round Norman arches made of brick and tufa blocks, a porous stone used by the Romans, probably taken from the remains of a Roman building nearby. Some of the early bricks used in the church were believed to be of Roman origin, but experts have pointed out that they are not the same size as Roman bricks and it is now thought that they were made locally about 1150. If this is so, this is the earliest surviving example of English brickwork.

It is likely that people worshipped on the top of this hill before the church was built, seeking shelter beneath a natural canopy provided by the "Gospel Oak", a tree reputed to have been thirteen hundred years old when it finally crumbled in 1953. It had the forethought to seed itself and a young oak has now grown in its place and taken the responsibility of sheltering the worshippers who still hold an annual service there during August. The remains of the old oak lie beneath the young tree, next to the church but just inside the grounds of Polstead Hall, a fine white Georgian building containing an earlier sixteenth century wing.

By tradition the youngest son of the Lord of the Manor succeeded to the title and land at Polstead, a custom known as "Borough English" as opposed to the more usual custom of primogeniture, where the elder son succeeds to the title. Gavelkind, the third alternative, where the wealth is divided equally between all the sons, is common in Kent.

Across the valley standing on the top of a spur of land which separates the Box from the Stour valley is Stoke-by-Nayland Church, whose massive tower, it seems, touches heaven itself. Stoke is a dream and a dreamy village, delightful in its solitude. Its half-timbered cottages, some plastered and pargetted, are clustered round the church to form the perfect image of an English village.

Queen Elizabeth I, England's greatest queen, was a descendant of Sir William Tendring, who inherited Tendring manor at Stoke in 1285. Alice, daughter of his great grandson, also Sir William Tendring, who fought at Agincourt, married Sir John Howard in 1398 and the Stoke estates thus passed into the Howard family. Their grandson, the first Duke of Norfolk, Sir John Howard, married Katharine Molyns whose tomb is in the church. A son, Thomas, born to them while they lived at Stoke, commanded the archers at the battle of Bosworth Field in 1485 and was responsible for defeating the Scots at Flodden in 1513. Two of Thomas's nieces, Anne Boleyn and Catherine Howard, were cousins and spent much of their early life at Tendring Hall overlooking the Stour before they lost their hearts and their heads to Henry VIII. Anne's daughter, Elizabeth, named after her grandmother Elizabeth Howard, became Queen of England.

Stoke is a favourite place of mine, where I like to sit outside the *Black Horse* and watch the locals play the ancient game of steel quoits. This game is taken very seriously in this part of the country, although it has died out elsewhere except in the north-east. It is played with a steel ring, just over seven inches in diameter and weighing 3¾ pounds, rounded on the top and flat or concave on the other side. The object is to throw the quoit over, or as near as possible to, a pin placed centrally in a bed of clay 18 yards from the thrower. The position of the pin is marked by pressing a small piece of paper on to the surface of the clay. A ringer, a quoit which encircles the pin and removed before the game continues, counts two points, while the quoit nearest to the pin counts one point. Quoits more than eighteen inches from the pin do not count and are removed, as are quoits lying on their backs—top side down.

The game has been played in England since the fourteenth century and is said to have developed from throwing the discus at the original Olympic games, although there is a strong connection with the game developed from throwing horseshoes. This would be appropriate, as the countryside round Stoke has been closely connected with the horse since the Normans brought over the European Great Horse at the time of the Conquest, grazing their animals on the meadows down at Dedham, where Leslie Mills now runs his "Heavy Horse Centre".

Suffolk Punches, the heavy, chestnut farm horses, a breed which came near to extinction twenty years ago, are kept by Roger and Cheryl Clark on their farm, Weylands. The farm is set in the midst of the most beautiful part of the Box valley, between Stoke and Thorington Street, in steep undulating hills described by Sir Alfred Munnings, as "the most lovely stretch of landscape in Suffolk." The horses earn their keep not only by working on their farm but by appearing in the county and national shows and by participating in com-

Right: Quoits being played at Stoke-by-Nayland.

Opposite: The annual service taking place in front of the old oak tree at Polstead.

Left: Cheryl Clark with a foal out of a Suffolk Punch.

mercial advertising promotions throughout the country. These powerful, lovable animals are a major attraction and very popular wherever they go.

It has been calculated that for a short haul horses are more economic than a tractor. Hopefully the increasing cost of fuel will encourage more of these horses to be kept on the farms. Down by the river the champion stallion of England grazes peacefully in his paddock while the Box flows gently past Thorington mill, its wheel no longer turned by the river, and under the main road near to the sixteenth-century Thorington Hall to join the Stour.

The attractive *Rose Inn* at Thorington Street makes use of local horse tradition by decorating its splendid oak-beamed bar with horse harness, leather and brasses.

The River Brett is fed by three headstreams. Near the source of the most westerly one, known by some as the River Brad, stands the market town of Lavenham, the finest remaining example of an English medieval town whose layout has altered little since the Middle Ages. The focal point of the town is a stone ecclesiastical cross made in 1501 and used since that time as the market cross, set in the market place which crowns the hill on which Lavenham is built. From here the streets run out radially down the hill. The half-timbered oak buildings with wattle and daub infilling have stood on their present sites since Tudor times and blend into and complement the countryside from which the building materials were taken.

Some of the Tudor buildings were brick faced to give the impression that they were Georgian. The front doors, opening directly on to the street, can be troublesome to the present occupiers, who sometimes find that tourists have entered their houses uninvited, if the door is left open during the summer months. A lady told me of the colonel living opposite her who left his house for a few moments to buy some cigarettes, to find on his return a family seated round his dining room table waiting to be served with afternoon tea.

The Guildhall of Corpus Christi, which occupies one side of the market square, became the centre of administration of the cloth industry, where merchant clothiers haggled over prices and pay, settled disputes and engaged their apprentices. When the cloth trade declined towards the end of the sixteenth century it became the Town Hall and then a bridewell. The Rev Rowland Taylor, rector of Hadleigh, spent two nights in it while on his way to the stake at Aldham Common outside Hadleigh in 1555. The Hall has been used as a workhouse, almshouses and a wool store and is now the property of the National Trust and is open to the public.

The old Wool Hall, now part of the *Swan Hotel*, was nearly lost to Lavenham when agents of the Princess Louise, a daughter of Queen Victoria, purchased the property on her behalf but without her knowledge. As the Hall was being dismantled and taken away on lorries, an enterprising parson, the Rev. Henry Taylor, hired a team of cyclists to follow the lorries to their destination, which proved to be Ascot, where the Hall was to be an addition to the Princess's cottage. When the reverend gentleman acquainted the princess with the facts, she agreed to return the Hall to Lavenham and have it restored at her own expense. It was then used for a while as a convalescent home for women railway workers, but then when the railway closed it was sold to become part of the *Swan Hotel*.

Lavenham Church, with its impressive tower over a hundred and forty feet high, was built in the Late Perpendicular style with stone brought from Barnack, Weldon and Clipsham in the Midlands and Caen stone from Normandy, to which was added some local flint and brick. The church, completed in 1525 amidst great rejoicing, was financed by the Lord of the Manor, John de Vere, and the Spring family, the rich clothiers of Lavenham.

Thomas Spring was a cloth merchant who had come down from Houghton-le-Spring near Durham and owned property at Lavenham and nearby Preston. He died in 1440, leaving money for the repair of the church of his day. His son, Thomas II, agreed to give 300 marks towards the first stage of the new church project and died the following year during which the foundations of the tower were laid. Thomas III (1456-1523), known as the

"Rich Clothier", continued the family support and the church was finally completed in 1525. Members of the Spring family remained in Lavenham until the end of the sixteenth century but descendants still show interest and support the magnificent structure. The de Veres and the Springs are many times recalled in the stonework of the building.

Whenever I stop and gaze with wonder at these great "wool-churches", I think of them, not as memorials to their rich benefactors' craving to buy a place in heaven, but as monuments to the children, who with their mothers, spun yarn on their distaffs from morning to dusk to help the family eke out a living and provided by their industry the wealth to build these churches.

Looking round Lavenham now it is difficult to appreciate that this was, and still is to some extent, an industrial town. The weaving of its famous Blue Cloth reached peak production towards the end of the fifteenth century at the time of the "Old Draperies" when Lavenham was printed large across the map of Europe. It was the wealth accrued by the clothiers at this time which financed the building of the present town and church.

Within a hundred years cloth weaving had become almost extinct, the large houses of the clothiers became derelict and many of the inhabitants migrated to America. Although some weaving of the new lighter fabrics, the "New Draperies', was undertaken, Lavenham now relied on the spinning of yarn, making use of the new spinning wheels, to supply the new weaving centres of Colchester, Norwich, London, and to a smaller extent Sudbury. The weaving tradition continued at Lavenham, however, into this century. During this time horsehair, straw, silk and coconut fibres have been made into materials of varying kinds. Today the town engages in light engineering (Stocko's in Barn Street) and in 1961 E. R. Holloway started to manufacture cosmetics in a building beside the river which was originally the first sugar beet factory in Great Britain, opened by James Duncan in 1868. Holloway's factory now incorporates the old railway station and goods yard (opened in 1865) and is one of the largest manufacturers of cosmetics in the country. The Lavenham Press has been established in the town since 1957 and stands opposite the point where the river leaves Lavenham for the pretty hamlets of Brent and Monks Eleigh. The company are well known printers of medical and other text books as well as high quality colour and general work. Part of the works and that occupied by the associated company, the publishers Terence Dalton Limited, was once a horse hair factory which manufactured the blinds for the Titanic.

Monks Eleigh, whose name derives from the Illeigh family who were the first Lords of the manors here, provides the passer-by with a picture-postcard view which has the village pump as its focal point. The green, surrounded by Tudor houses, slopes gently up to the church. It was here that I met David Randall, one of the country's leading experts in the propagation of orchids for the cut flower market, who grows the most beautiful orchids under glass at his home, Highlands Hall.

David first became interested in growing orchids as a hobby to interest his children when he was the general manager of an Anglo-American chemical company in Northumberland. He started with a hundred plants given to him by a friend, and soon gave up his job to concentrate on the commercial cultivation of orchids by meristem propagation, test tube reproduction, which he developed from the work of Professor George Morel, of Paris University.

Meristem propagation does not depend on seeds or cuttings or any other conventional method of reproduction but is achieved by removing the growing cells of the plants, *apical meristems,* which form and divide just behind the growing tip of the roots and stems. This is done under a microscope—the meristem is about the size of a pin head—in clinically clean conditions. It is

Orchids grown by David Randall at his Monks Eleigh nurseries.

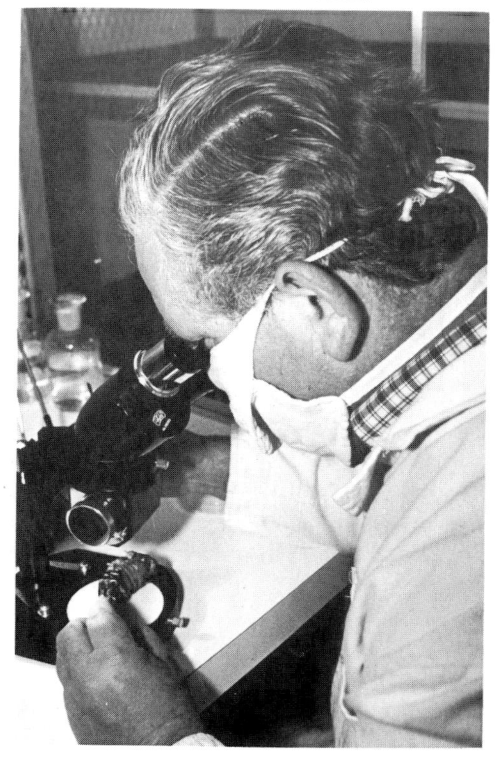

David Randall removing the meristem from the shoot of an orchid corm.

then placed in a special nutrient in which it continues to grow and divide, producing groups of cells known as protocorms, which eventually polarise, producing stems and roots, to form small identical plants. Five years later the first flowers appear. David Randall has named one of his most beautiful orchid hybrids after his adopted village, Monks Eleigh, whose beauty complements his flowers.

At Chelsworth, considered by many to be the prettiest village in Suffolk, the river from Monks Eleigh is joined by a stream coming south from Brettenham known locally as the Wagger or Walsham's River. It is also referred to as the River Brett, and now flows between tree-lined banks through the centre of the village and under a delightful hump-backed bridge to create an idyllic rustic scene.

Beyond Chelsworth the river is joined by a third tributary, also referred to as the Brett at Nedging mill. It has its source a couple of miles to the north in the elongated village of Hitcham where the Reverend John Stevens Henslow was the Rector from 1837 to 1861. He is best known as the teacher, friend and inspiration of Charles Darwin but for me, a science teacher, his greatest achievements were the introduction of Botany as a school subject and the formulation of the principles of modern science education, commonly referred to as "scientific method", which we so closely follow today.

John Stevens Henslow was born at Maidstone in Kent on 6th February 1796, the eldest of eleven children. At the age of nine he left the Free Mathematical School at Rochester to enter a boarding school at Camberwell, where he received instruction in natural history from his drawing master and was privately tutored by Dr Leach from the British Museum. He graduated from St John's College, Cambridge, as a mathematician in 1818 and was soon appointed Professor of Mineralogy (1822). Five years later he succeeded to the Chair of Botany and immediately set about improving the standards of teaching at the university.

Science teaching is not simply a matter of passing on information but is a process of inducing pupils carefully to observe either experiments or nature, from which they draw conclusions which can be tested by further experiments. Although we think of this scientific method as being new, it was introduced by Henslow at Cambridge more than a hundred and fifty years ago.

Charles Darwin was one of the first to put Henslow's ideas into practice when he sailed on board the *Beagle*, under the command of Captain Fitzroy, as the unpaid naturalist accompanying a Government survey of the South American coast. Darwin had been persuaded by Henslow to take the position on the *Beagle*. Darwin's observations of the wildlife, particularly on the Galapagos Islands, led him to his theory of the Origin of Species, which brought him into conflict with the Book of Genesis and the teaching of the Church at that time.

The hump-backed bridge over the Brett at Chelsworth.

Henslow was ordained priest in 1824 and for a while was the Rector of Cholsey-cum-Moulsford, in Berkshire, before taking up what was then the Crown living at Hitcham in 1837.

The tastefully restored and well-kept cottages now give an air of prosperity to the Stour villages, but it was not always so. When Henslow took over the parish there was considerable unemployment and social distress amongst the labouring class, who existed on a diet of potatoes and bread, while their children from the age of six would work in the fields picking stones, weeding or pulling turnips to earn perhaps a shilling a week.

The philanthropic rector relieved their poverty by providing the people with allotments on which they could grow food for themselves and organised a variety of self-help clubs including a coal club, clothing and medical clubs financed by the members and the rector. Ploughing matches and horticultural shows were organised to increase the skills and enthusiasm of the artisans. It was not long before Henslow built a school house and employed a school mistress, financed mainly from his own pocket, opening Hitcham Parish School in 1841.

Henslow taught the children his favourite subject, botany, in a voluntary class he held on Monday afternoons, and he endeavoured to develop in his pupils the scientific approach which he had pioneered while he was at Cambridge. Unfortunately he also insisted that his pupils learnt the correct systematic botanical terminology and words such as *Angiospermous* and *Thalamifloral* soon appeared on their spelling lists. Henslow's scientific teaching brought the school national esteem, which resulted in the Rector being employed as tutor to the children of Queen Victoria.

In 1854 the first qualified teacher was appointed and the monitorial system introduced; a method by which pupils who had reached the age of

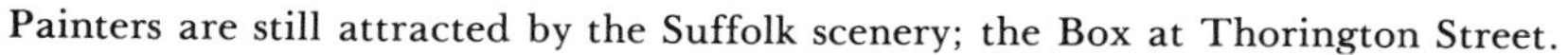
Painters are still attracted by the Suffolk scenery; the Box at Thorington Street.

thirteen received extra tuition in return for instructing the younger pupils. This developed into the pupil-teacher apprenticeship scheme whereby monitors could sit an external examination every year for five years to become qualified teachers. It is a system which has much to commend it. As a result Hitcham school provided many of the qualified teachers required in this area. The first was Harriet Sewell, a pupil of the school who became a governess and maintained her interest in botany as she travelled the world.

Henslow also applied himself to adult education, encouraged his parishioners to learn to read and provided them with a library of a hundred books. He also persuaded the farmers, who were generally opposed to his ideas of educating the lower classes, to apply scientific principles to improve their farming, especially to make use of chemical fertilisers—the professor discovered large deposits of coprolite, a fossilised dung containing a high proportion of calcium phosphate, when he went to Felixstowe.

When Sir William Hooker created Kew gardens he was assisted by Henslow, who planned the herbarium and the museum. A marble bust at Kew commemorates his work there. Frances Henslow, the professor's daughter, married Joseph Hooker, Sir William's son. Henslow also established the museum at Ipswich and took advantage of the newly inaugurated railways to take his parishioners on excursions to Ipswich, Norwich, Cambridge and London for their further education. The rector died in 1861 and in 1883 the church porch at Hitcham was restored in his memory, but I like to think of his book, *The Flora of Suffolk*, compiled with the help of his pupils in the fields around Hitcham, as the true memorial to this remarkable man.

From Hitcham the stream works its way south through the old woollen town of Bildeston before joining the River Brett, which now accepts the waters of the Carsey stream from Lindsey and Kersey before it comes to the Royal town of Hadleigh.

Bildeston was a woollen town at the time of the "Old Draperies" and famous for its blankets. The old weavers' cottages add character to its main street, through which the traffic thunders, leaving undisturbed Edward Rotherham who is buried in the churchyard on a hillside outside the village. He was the Commander of Admiral Collingwood's flagship, The *Royal Sovereign*, at the battle of Trafalgar. He died of apoplexy whilst visiting his friends the Wilsons at Bildeston House.

The Carsey stream, said to give its name to the best known and possibly the prettiest village in England, Kersey,* is its centre of attraction as it trickles across the ford at the bottom of the main street, its work of washing wool to make Kerseymere having long been finished. This was a cheap heavy cloth used for making men's clothing, while further upstream at Lindsey they made lighter fabrics for ladies' wear, the lindseys, a name which still classifies some types of cloth.

*According to *The Oxford Dictionary of Place Names* Kersey means cress island. The stream was noted for the watercress that grew in it.

The river at Hadleigh is deep and wide, held back by the old sluice of Toppesfield mill to enhance a picturesque promenade beneath a canopy of sheltering trees. The ancient town square stands on the east bank near to Toppesfield Bridge, named after the manor to which it originally belonged, remote and secluded from the commercial bustle along Hadleigh High Street. Here in this pretty corner of the town was buried Guthrum, who died in 890 whilst visiting the town. Guthrum was defeated by King Alfred of Wessex, but agreeing to embrace Christianity was allowed to rule East Anglia.

Towards the end of the twelfth century the tiny wooden church in which Guthrum was buried was replaced by a larger stone building whose tower still survives in the present church, which was built mostly during the fifteenth century. The tall, slender and elegant spire which surmounts the tower is, at its apex, 135 feet from the ground and it is also a survival from the thirteenth century, although its wooden frame was recovered with lead in 1926. The bell hanging above its clock face is probably the oldest in the country. The Angelus Bell, as it is known, has been estimated from the style of lettering on it, the words *AVE MARIA GRACIA PLENA DOMINUS TECUM* cast the wrong way round, to be over six hundred years old.

Hadleigh had been foremost in responding to the Protestant ideas of Martin Luther, which were disseminated by a small group of Cambridge intellectuals, and in 1538 Hadleigh Church became the first in which the Mass was read in English.

In 1544 Archbishop Cranmer appointed Rowland Taylor to be the Rector of Hadleigh. Taylor had married when he was only sixteen, fathered nine children and was ordained a priest in 1541. The Protestant movement gathered momentum through the reigns of Henry VIII and Edward VI until the Catholic Queen Mary came to the throne in 1553. Rowland Taylor was arrested after he had attempted to prevent the Latin Mass being read in his church in front of a stone altar the Catholics had erected for the purpose. Taylor was taken to London to appear before Stephen Gardiner, a Suffolk man who was Bishop of Winchester and the Lord Chancellor. The Rector persisted in advocating the English form of the Mass and rejected the doctrine of transubstantiation, and was condemned to death by burning. He was brought back to Hadleigh, stopping possibly at Sudbury and at Lavenham gaol on the way back, taken to Aldham Common just outside Hadleigh on 9th February, 1555, stood in a barrel of pitch and tied to the stake. Mercifully a bystander killed him with a blow to the head before the flames could reach him.

An unhewn stone with the inscription, ANNO 1555 D TAYLOR · IN · DEFENDING · THAT · WAS · GOOD · AT · THIS · PLAS · LEFT · HIS · BLODE, marks the place of his martyrdom. Richard Yeoman, Taylor's curate, suffered a similar fate a year later when he was discovered hiding in an

Hadleigh church and the Deanery Tower.

upper room at the Guildhall. He was taken to Norwich and there burnt at the stake on the 10th July, 1558.

On the adjacent side of the Square to the church stands the castellated brick Deanery Tower, completed in 1495 by the Rector of Hadleigh, William Pykenham. It was originally intended to be a gateway to a more splendid residence nearer the river, but the Rector died before realising his ambition. Opposite the church stands the three-storeyed timber-framed Guildhall with two overhanging jetties, a reminder that Hadleigh was the town with the largest production of cloth in Suffolk at the time of the Old Draperies. Today

The memorial to Dr Rowland Taylor and his curate, the Rev Richard Yeoman, and, below, the inscription.

Mark this rude stone where Taylor dauntlefs stood,
Where Zeal infuriate drank the Martyr's blood
Hadleigh! That day how many a tearful eye
Saw thy lov'd Pastor dragg'd a Victim by;
Still scattering gifts and blefsings as He past.
To the Blind Pair his farewell alms were cast:
His clinging Flock e'en here around him pray'd
As thou hast aided us, Be God thine Aid".
Nor taunts, nor bribe of mitred rank, nor stake.
Nor blows, nor flames, his heart of firmnefs shake:
Serene his folded hands his upward eyes
Like holy Stephen's, seek the opening skies:
There fix'd in rapture, his prophetic sight
Views Truth dawn clear on England's Bigot night:
Triumphant Saint! He bow'd and kifs'd the rod.
And soar'd on Seraph wing to meet his God.

Hadleigh is the centre of a thriving community. A modern industrial estate on the outskirts of the town provides local employment, while its shops, many housed in delightful medieval buildings decorated with colourful pargetting, provide a pleasant shopping centre.

The Brett bows out of Hadleigh under Toppesfield Bridge, the overflow water tumbling over a small weir to form a stream which now meanders its way south, forming a pretty corner at Layham mill and another at Shelley before it joins the Stour behind Higham church. Layham mill was built about 1906 to replace an older mill which was burnt down and is one of the last working watermills as well as the last to be built in Suffolk.

Giffords Hall, standing on an elevated position between the Box and the Brett just south of Shelley, is one of the finest mansions of Henry VIII's period still remaining. It was the seat of the staunchly Roman Catholic Mannock family. Unfortunately it is enclosed in wooded parkland which obscures it from view.

The river is at its best as it passes through the meadows at Higham, which with the surrounding undulating hills creates a delightful part of the Stour valley. Higham situated in its midst maintains the equine tradition of this pretty place by providing its well known point-to-point race-course, while on the opposite side of the river, high on the hillside, stands Langham Church with its strong associations with the artist John Constable.

CHAPTER SEVEN

The Dedham Vale

IT HAD been my original intention while writing this book to walk the complete length of the Stour along its banks from its source to the sea, but this proved to be impossible because of lack of access to many parts of the river.

However, the seven-mile country walk across the fields from Langham Church through the Dedham Vale to the estuary at Manningtree was more than adequate compensation for my initial disappointment. This is Constable Country,* named after another of East Anglia's great artists, John Constable (1776-1837), who was born and brought up in the valley. His paintings, which have immortalised the scenery of the Stour Valley (or did the scenery immortalise his paintings?), made people aware, perhaps for the first time, of the beauty of their own countryside. There can be few homes in England without a Constable reproduction framed on the walls, on a plate, lampshade, table mat or something.

Of the prospect of his own popularity Constable wrote,

"My art flatters nobody by imitation;
it courts nobody by smoothness;
it tickles nobody by petiteness;
it is without fal-de-fal or fiddle-me-dee,
how then can I hope to be popular."

Langham church stands high on the hillside on the Essex side of the river, known as Gun Hill from the name of an inn which stood on the hill when the main road passed that way, opposite to Higham on the north bank. From the tall, square church tower, built intermittently between the thirteenth and fifteenth centuries, one has commanding views of the valley as far as the estuary and beyond to the shipping at Harwich. It was this vantage point that Constable used for his painting *Dedham Vale*, which he completed in 1828 and described as "probably my best painting". Adjacent to the church and just below it stands the seventeenth-century Church Farm, the subject of Constable's *Glebe Farm*, which he painted in 1827 as a memorial to his friend Dr John Fisher, Bishop of Salisbury.

The artist had first met John Fisher at Langham, while the doctor was Rector of Langham. Fisher was prominent in fashionable society and was

*Designated an area of outstanding natural beauty by the Countryside Commission in 1967.

referred to as the "King's Fisher" because of his association with King George III. The rector visited his Langham parish only infrequently. He was appointed Bishop of Salisbury in 1807 and four years later invited Constable to stay with him. Constable was introduced to the Bishop's nephew, also John Fisher, archdeacon. The two men became life-long friends of the artist and a source of strength to him.

John spent his honeymoon at the archdeacon's house in Osmington, Dorset. Langham must have held many romantic memories for John Constable, for it was here that he met and secretly courted Maria Bicknell, his future wife.

Outside in the churchyard, sheltered by tall, majestic horse chestnut trees, stands a small, square, brick, ugly building which was built in 1832 by the then rector, Dr Hurlock, for the daily instruction of poor girls in the parish. The inscription on the school reads;

> "This building is designed for the daily instruction of poor girls of this parish in the principles of the Church of England: and for the reception of the poor and infirm between the services on the Sabbath.
>
> The examination of the children and teacher is vested in the Rector for the time being exclusively".

Payment by results in those days. I wonder if the teacher passed!

The Reverend Dr J. T. Hurlock who built the school was the son of the Rev. Jas Hurlock, who acted as curate for the parish and carried out the duties of the absent Rector, Dr John Fisher.

A splendid avenue of lime trees leads round the corner from the church to Langham Hall. The original manor was, according to tradition, held by Sir Walter Tyrrel who was believed to have killed King William II in the New Forest on 2nd August, 1100.

One can now follow this footpath and others all the way to Epping Forest on the outskirts of London. It is a route for walkers pioneered by the Council for the Protection of Rural England and admirably described in J. V. C. Clarke's booklet *The Essex Way*. Happily our path is shorter, and lies in the opposite direction, returning past the church and taking the footpath which descends the hill and then bears right over the fields to cross the Stour at Stratford St Mary.

This is a pretty part of the river, lined with trees and flowing along the side of the village street. The barge horses rested here while the barge was taken through the locks and the bargee took the opportunity to quench his thirst in the *Swan* on the opposite side of the road.

Stratford St Mary is quiet now, having been by-passed in 1976 by a new dual carriageway section of the A12 from London to Lowestoft. The 2.75 miles of the Stratford by-pass, with its ten bridges, cost a million and a quarter pounds. Although Stratford St Mary owed much of its wealth to the wool trade of the Middle Ages, it also enjoyed prominence as an important stopping off place for travellers between London and Norfolk ever since Roman times. Its name comes from *Via Strata*, Roman for paved street, which forded the Stour at Stratford. The Romans also had a staging post on Gun Hill just outside the village, known as *Ad Ansam* or "At the handle" of the Stour, referring to the shape of the bend of the river at this point.

From the Middle Ages onwards drovers from Norfolk walked their geese, turkeys and other animals along this route to London to reach the capital in time for Christmas. According to Defoe more than 300 droves a year would cross the Stratford bridge, each drove consisting of up to a thousand birds. The webbed feet of the geese were protected by walking them through tar and grit, while the turkeys were often fitted with leather boots.

The *Black Horse*, one of four inns serving the traveller in Stratford St Mary, was associated with the highwayman Matthew Keys, who finding himself with insufficient money to pay his bill left behind his watch, sword and pistol.

Le Talbooth restaurant, which enjoys a considerable reputation for its food, stands beside the Stour at the bottom of Gun Hill, Dedham.

Le Talbooth is a very fine but very much restored seventeenth-century building which stands beside the Stour at the southern end of the village, where successive bridges have carried the road over the river. The Talbooth, known by this name since 1659, was a building where merchandise was weighed and tolls collected for the upkeep of the bridge.* There was also a mill house and a smithy here, and later a lime-kiln and a wharf were built on the site. Today the *Talbooth* houses a fine and well-known restaurant.

An old toll house built with the bridge constructed in 1787 displayed a sign, which read

> Rest, drivers, rest on this steep hill.
> Dumb beasts pray use with all good will.
> Goad not, scourge not, with thonged whips,
> Let not one curse escape your lips.

*The Talbooth and the wooden bridge across the Stour are featured in Constable's *The Valley of the Stour and Dedham*.

Two alternative paths follow the Stour from Stratford to Dedham, one either side of the river. The Essex path is reached by crossing over the A12 by the road bridge from the *Talbooth* and then following the road to the main entrance of the Dedham Vale Hotel, opposite which the path disappears into a copse to follow the river past the pumping station to Dedham High Street. The prettier and pleasanter path on the Suffolk side commences between the *Black Horse* and the *Talbooth*, passing through a tunnel underneath the A12. It then emerges on the other side to follow the river through a wide, flat valley, filled with luscious green pasture until it reaches Dedham mill. Here Constable selected a point looking across the mill pool, with the lock gates to his right and the church tower behind them, to paint his *Dedham Mill*.

"I wish we had a small house here," remarked John Constable about Dedham in 1821. It is a sentiment expressed by my wife every time we go to Dedham to do our weekly shopping. Of all the wool towns and villages along the Stour, Dedham ranks first in our affection. Its attraction lies only partly within the picturesque and historic High Street, on one side of which stands its fine Perpendicular Gothic church and tower, so often included by Constable in his paintings.

The two historic inns have provided excellent sustenance beneath oak beams for two hundred years or more. The *Marlborough Head* standing on the corner of Mill Street and High Street was, together with Church House, formerly Cheese House, originally a fifteenth-century clearing house for woollen goods belonging to a rich clothier. Its upper floor, well ventilated with mullioned windows fitted with adjustable shutter flaps, was used for storage. The ground floor had sides open to the market and was used as a wool hall, and the cellars contained the large wooden vats in which the cloth was dyed. By 1660 the wool trade had declined and there was a change of use when, for a time, part of it became an apothecary's shop. It was then reconditioned and became an inn in 1704, the year the Duke of Marlborough scored his famous victory over the French at Blenheim, the inn being named after the victorious Duke.

The *Sun Inn*, formerly *Bards*, was built a century after the *Marlborough* and gained prominence during the era of the stage coach. Its high archway with a bracketed roof beam permitted the entrance into the courtyard of coaches piled high with luggage and outside passengers. A rare example of an outside roofed staircase, once leading to a dovecote, rests against the inn wall, while a wooden gallery once surrounded the courtyard. It must have made a pretty picture.

Although this small country village in the midst of a farming community continues to receive thousands of visitors every year, it has not succumbed to commercial pressure but accommodates its guests without them spoiling the beauty they have come to view. The real charm of Dedham is that it is still a

The annual bank holiday market, held in front of the old Grammar School at Dedham, seen towards the right of the picture.

flourishing community with a regular pulse of its own, which beats undisturbed by the periodic intrusions of tourists.

Dedham owes its position on the Stour to the Black Brook, a name which is supposed to have originated from blanc, the French for white. A clear case of white being black! The brook encircles the village from the south before crossing under the eastern end of Dedham High Street to flow into the Stour near the bridge. Its clear water was a valuable asset in the woollen dyeing process.

The ford at Dedham was the lowest crossing point of the Stour in Saxon times, and here the Dydda family settled in the fork of the two rivers, giving their name to the settlement. After the Conquest the two manors at Dedham were held by numerous lords, the best known being Sir John Fastolf (1378-1459), who went to France with Henry V during the Hundred Years War. In 1429 he was made a Knight of the Garter for his defeat of the French at the Battle of Herrings, fought at Rouvrai and so called because the convoy Sir John was

defending was carrying Lenten provisions, mainly herrings, to the English army at neighbouring Orleans.

Later at the battle of Patay he was accused of cowardice for leaving the battlefield without reason, but this allegation was later rescinded and the gallant knight returned with full honours to his manors at Dedham and his home at Caister castle. It was from the alleged incident of cowardice that Shakespeare created Falstaff, the companion to Prince Hal in *Henry IV*.

Like so many other places along the Stour, Dedham became part of the property of Catherine of Aragon on her marriage to Henry VIII and then passed in turn to Anne Boleyn, Jane Seymour and Anne of Cleves, after which much of the property reverted to the State or the Duchy of Lancaster. The Duchy barn at the corner of the recreation ground, now used as a tourist information centre by the Council for the Protection of Rural England, is so named because it belongs to the Duchy of Lancaster.

The development of the cloth industry in Dedham followed a similar

HOTEL
THE SUN HOTEL
ENTRANCE
NO

pattern to that of the other wool towns along the Stour but remained in small domestic units, never being dominated by a large monopoly such as the Springs of Lavenham. It depended on Colchester for the distribution of its finished cloth, which under the influence of its parent town consisted mainly of bays, light twilled worsted, and says, a fine serge-like cloth.

The town reached its zenith towards the end of the fifteenth century when the great wool house complexes at the *Marlborough Head,* Castle House and Southfields were constructed. These were not factories containing looms but suites of buildings which included the clothier's dwelling, offices, storehouses and sometimes vats for dyeing the cloth. Southfields, which stands on the Black Brook at the far end of the cricket field away from the church, is unique in being built round a quadrangle in a similar style to a Tudor mansion by a member of the Sherman family about 1500. Some of the great wealth accumulated by the clothiers, at Dedham the Webbe and Gurdon families were prominent, was used to finance the erection of the great wool churches. The one at Dedham, built from 1492 with stone brought up the Stour from Caen in Normandy, is a fine example, its tower forming the focal point of many of Constable's paintings.

When Queen Elizabeth I ascended the throne one of her first proclamations was to suppress independent religious belief and discussion by banning preaching from the pulpit. To promulgate her official religious line, which was still basically Roman Catholic even though she, and not the Pope, was now head of the Church, she relied on carefully prepared homilies being read out by officiating ministers during divine service. Perhaps this was just as well, as the clergy at this time had a poor reputation. To quote Gerald Rendall,* a past vicar of Dedham,

> "The Tudor clergy were as a body grossly illiterate; neither their training nor their intellectual resources fitted them to be preachers. 'Hardly one in a hundred is both able and willing to preach the word of God'."

To overcome both these difficulties devoutly religious people, either as individuals or as groups such as the trade gilds, financed lecturers to preach the word of God as they understood it and believed it to be. Needless to say the views expressed by the lecturers were frequently hostile to those held by the Established Church, which attempted to silence them, and often succeeded.

Many of the lecturers were sympathetic to the Puritan movement, strong in Dedham as elsewhere along the Stour. Their aim initially was not to repudiate the Church but to bring about reform within and to purify it.

One of the longest surviving Lectureships is the one at Dedham, which was instituted about 1578 and financed by quarterly subscriptions from the

◀ Dedham High Street, with the *Sun* on the left and the churchyard wall on the right.

***Dedham in History.*

Boats for hire on the river at Dedham, where a boatyard was building large sea-going yachts not many years ago.

inhabitants, administered by local trustees. The responsibilities of the appointed lecturer were to preach on Sunday afternoon, at which time he would also catechise the children, but his main lecture took place on market day. An hour before Dedham market opened the punctual bell was rung. The market then reached from the *Sun Inn* to the *Marlborough Head.*

Such was the popularity enjoyed by the lecturers that when one of them, John Rogers, known as Roaring Rogers because of the manner of his delivery, died in 1636, the gallery of the church was so packed with people at his funeral that it collapsed under their weight. It was considered a miracle that no one was injured. The galleries were finally removed from the church in 1862.

William Burkitt, probably the other most famous lecturer at Dedham, rejuvenated the Lectureship when he was appointed to the post in 1692. He realised that it could no longer continue by private subscription alone and inaugurated an endowment policy to maintain it. He is also noted for his great work, *The Commentary,* in which he wrote explanatory notes on the four gospels for the benefit of "the plain and unlearned reader". The work was published in 1724, twenty-one years after his death, and by 1760 it had run into its fifteenth edition.

Burkitt was the last of the great national figures who held office at Dedham, although the Lectureship continued until 1918, during which time several of the headmasters of the Grammar School and some of the Dedham Vicars held the office. After 1918 the title was incorporated into that of the

Vicar of Dedham, the lectures now being given during a weeknight service in Lent or Advent.

The finest sermon I heard at Dedham did not come from the clergy but from a robin which had been enticed into the church by the seed and grain lying among the harvest festival decorations. Dedham church is noted for its beautiful and professional flower decorations displayed during the church festivals. The robin flew on to the pulpit microphone, puffed out its feathers and proceeded to fill the church with its song in praise of the Lord. The church was full at the time and the many visitors stopped, turned and listened for a good five minutes. Few parsons I have heard have such commanding eloquence. That little bird's message came over very clearly to me.

Inside the church a commemorative pew, on which is carved the first Great Seal of the American Republic bearing the emblem of an eagle clutching at thirteen arrows, representing the original number of American States, links New England with the mother country. Puritans from Dedham probably accompanied both John Winthrop from Groton and Samuel Sherman of Dedham, when they set out for America in 1630 and 1634 to found the State of Massachusetts. General W. T. Sherman, the Civil War commander, claimed descent from Samuel Sherman.

Some of the colonists settled at a place they named Contentment, twenty miles from Boston, but they later renamed it Dedham after their native village. In 1967 this village contributed over a thousand pounds for the restoration of the church in the village from which their own took its name. Appropriately another pew commemorates the conquering of space by the Americans when they were the first to land men on the moon.

A boulder placed against the outside of the south wall of the church is in memory of Edward Ward, ploughman. One legend described him as something of an uncouth reprobate who was struck down and hit, presumably by the boulder, on a hot summer's day for his sins. The more likely explanation is that his plough struck the stone while he was working in the adjoining fields and he decided there and then to have it for his tombstone.

That Dedham possessed a grammar school is well known because of its famous, if somewhat reticent pupil, John Constable, who came to the school at Dedham having had some very unpleasant experiences at the boarding grammar school at Lavenham. Since the middle of the sixteenth century Dedham possessed both an English or Writing School in which the teaching of reading, writing and arithmetic were undertaken and a Grammar School for instruction in Latin and Greek grammar, hence its name. Its high academic reputation attracted the wealthy to settle in the village so that their sons could attend the local school; a situation which persists in many other places at the present time. This probably helped to maintain the prosperity of Dedham after its weaving industry declined.

The first school at Dedham was founded some time during the middle of the sixteenth century by the wealthy traders, weavers, yeomen and farmers for the education of their children who occupied premises provided by Dame Joan Clarke. It was to this school in 1571 that William Littlebury, a rich clothier, gave an endowment for the education of twenty boys from poor homes in the villages of Dedham, Ardleigh, Much Bromley, Bradfield and Stratford, but they had to be literate before they entered the school, where they studied the Latin and Greek grammar.

In 1575 the Queen gave the school its Royal Charter and it became known as The Free Grammar School of Queen Elizabeth in Dedham. Headmasters were appointed from either Oxford or Cambridge universities, with which the school had strong links, and an usher, or assistant teacher, was appointed and paid by the headmaster. The school day began in summer at 6 a.m. and continued until five in the afternoon, an hour being taken off each end of the day in winter. School finished at three in the afternoon on Saturday, when an hour was devoted to learning the catechism ready for Sunday.

The masters and boys were required to attend both services on Sunday and sat together in one place with their books and pens. A Godly prayer, approved by the school governors, marked the opening and closing of each school day. Archery provided the main relaxation and each pupil was required to have his own bow, shafts and shooting glove. It must have been difficult to find sufficient poor scholars with the required academic background and with the means to pay for the school accoutrements as well as their lodgings in the village. As a result the school gradually changed from a day school for the instruction of a few poor boys to a boarding school for the education of the sons of the gentry and professional classes.

The new school building, which still stands next to the church and opposite the *Marlborough Head*, was built in 1731 under the direction of the headmaster, Thomas Grimwood, whose name is perpetuated on a wall plaque outside the school. It was his son, Dr Thomas Lechmere Grimwood, who taught Constable.

By 1755 the poor free scholars had been separated from the fee-paying élite and made to feel their inferior position. The free scholars were taught separately, possibly in another building, and were not permitted the use of the playground or playing fields, which were rented by the headmaster for the benefit of the fee-paying scholars. Although the school was reorganised in 1873 to provide a more liberal and practical education, it began to run into financial difficulties and when a polluted water supply led to an outbreak of diphtheria in 1889 the school was temporarily closed; it never reopened.

Edmund Sherman founded the English or Writing School in 1599, twenty-eight years after Littlebury had given the original school its endowment which was to alter its function from an elementary to a Grammar school.

Sherman gave a tenement for the occupation of a schoolmaster, who was committed to teaching the children to read and write. At this time the instruction was free. The school house was rebuilt about the same time as that of the Grammar school, 1731, and in a similar style, displaying a very ornate brick Georgian facade which still faces the north porch of the church across the High Street. It is the house with the sundial. Eight boarders resided in the attic, while a similar number of day boys between the ages of ten and thirteen were given free instruction. The school closed in 1872 and the building was then used as a private school for girls for a short time.

From Dedham the two footpaths continue on either side of the river to Flatford mill. The Essex path commences at the east end of Dedham High Street, crossing the meadows behind Dedham Hall to reach the meandering Stour which it follows between the pollarded willows. Our path on the Suffolk side is regained by returning down Mill Lane and crossing the road bridge, from where the path follows the river for a short distance before turning away across the meadows to Fen bridge and up a leafy lane to East Bergholt. It was this lane which Constable made the subject of his painting *The Cornfield*. The small boy in the red blouse quenching his thirst from the stream by the lane could well have been the boy Constable as he went this way to school at Dedham. I was told that this was the direct route taken by the horse-drawn Royal Mail coaches from Bergholt to Dedham, although there is no sign now of a suitable track beyond Fen bridge. From the top of the hill at the end of this lane can be seen some fine views of the Stour valley with the church towers of Dedham and Stratford St Mary dwarfed in the distance.

East Bergholt Church has no tower or belfry. Its five bells are the heaviest bells currently being rung in England and the oldest, Gabrielle, dates from 1450. They are housed in a wooden bell cage in the churchyard, which is a fine example of late medieval timberwork. The present church, dating from 1350, probably possessed both a tower and a belfry but they became unsafe and either fell down or were demolished. A new tower was commenced in 1525 at the expense, it is believed, of Cardinal Wolsey, the son of an Ipswich butcher, who became the influential friend and adviser of Henry VIII.

The Cardinal had suppressed many religious houses, including Dodnash priory at Bergholt, to finance the construction of his colleges at Cambridge and Ipswich. In order to pacify the outraged villagers, Wolsey promised to finance their new tower. When he failed to obtain an annulment of Henry's marriage to Catherine he fell from grace and the village lost its money. Another local legend tells of the Devil pulling down each night the work which had been completed on the tower during the day until the builders gave up the unequal struggle. The decline of the wool trade has also been blamed for the lack of funds, but it is most likely that this shortage was due to the reluctance of the wealthy, after the Reformation, to leave their money for church building, which was often plundered for religious reasons or personal gain. They left their money instead for the sustenance of the poor.

It is not certain at what date, although 1531 has been suggested, the villagers decided to house their bells in a temporary cage but as late as 1541 legacies were still being left for the completion of the tower. The cage was originally erected on the eastern side of the churchyard near to the tower, but the family at the Old Hall opposite complained of the noise so it was moved to its present position at a parishioner's expense. The five bells are supported at ground level by a heavy wooden frame with the mouth of the bells facing upwards. A bell is rung by pushing it off balance so that it falls into the pit, its momentum, assisted by a push on the headstock by the ringer, moves it through a semi-circle until it is again poised upright on its headstock, ready for the process to be repeated.

Before clocks and watches were commonplace, the church bells marked the important times of the day. At Bergholt a rising bell was sounded at 5 a.m. and the curfew bell indicated that it was bedtime. The harvest bell was rung at eight in the morning and seven in the evening. At these times grain could be gleaned from the fields. The ringer of the harvest bell was paid by a collection contributed by the gleaners. The bells were also rung one hour before morning

service and Evensong, which was in the afternoon, calling the parishioners to worship at the appointed hour.

Bells ring for joy and eke for sadness,
For solemn Requiem,
Or in the marriage Peal of Gladness,
Do thou like them
Fitly employ the voice
The Scripture precept keep,
Rejoice with them that do rejoice
And weep with them that weep.

From a verse displayed inside the Bergholt bell cage.

Next to the church once stood the red-brick house where John Constable was born on 11th June, 1776. Nothing now remains of his home apart from the stables and the railings on which has been recently attached a modest metal plaque inscribed,

Site of East Bergholt House,
Childhood home of John Constable R.A.
1776-1837

Opposite: The medieval bell cage in the churchyard at East Bergholt.

Right: Ringing the bells at East Bergholt, showing the unique method used.

Stour House, East Bergholt, formerly the home of Mr Randolph Churchill, son of the famous wartime Prime Minister.

The artist was born into a family which had farmed in the Stour valley for generations. His grandfather came from Bures and his father Golding inherited the lands and property at Flatford from his uncle Abram, and later acquired the mill at Dedham. Golding met Ann Watts on one of his visits to London and married her before her nineteenth birthday. They moved into Flatford mill, where they had three children, Ann, Martha and Golding. They decided that the place was too small for their expanding family and had their spacious home built up the hill at East Bergholt. John was the first child to be born in their new home, and he was followed by two more children, Mary and Abram, bringing the total complement to six. It was John's idyllic boyhood beside the Stour, with its natural beauty and bustling activity in the mills and on the barges, that inspired and influenced him as a painter and provided the subjects for his paintings in the years to come.

John Dunthorne, the village plumber, glazier and confirmed atheist, was Constable's first painting companion, from who he learnt to paint in the open air away from the studio so as to capture the natural moods of light and shade. John Dunthorne's cottage, proudly wearing a coat of pink wash, still stands next to the entrance of Constable's old home while opposite, above the shop, is the room the painter once hired as a studio.

The life and works of England's greatest artist are well documented and I would recommend the reader to Freda Constable's lucid biography of her husband's ancestor. Although I have little artistic inclination, I find I can repeatedly return to Constable's pictures of the Stour and each time find in them something new and invigorating. His works are equally important as a commentary on the social and industrial life of the Stour in his time, which in many respects, especially for the wealthy, was better and more settled than our own.

The path by the Stour is regained at Flatford Mill by returning to the church, leaving Stour House, the home for a time of Randolph Churchill, on the right and descending the hill to the river, leaving on the left the ugly grey buildings of Old Hall, built on the site of King Harold's personal Royal Manor, then the largest in East Suffolk. The present buildings were for a time used as a Convent by a community of Benedictine Nuns and then by the Friars for training their novices. They now house a commune.

Flatford Mill, the lock, Willy Lott's cottage, formerly known as Gibeon's farm, and the barges were the most popular subjects for Constable's brush; *The Haywain* is undoubtedly the best known. Other pictures of this place include *Flatford Mill, Boat Building at Flatford Mill, The Leaping Horse* and *Valley Farm*, which is another view of Willy Lott's cottage and not of the picturesque timbered building nearby, which is also called Valley Farm. I was told by a former occupier that Constable never sketched or painted Valley Farm, and they presumed that Constable could not have liked the people there.

At Flatford I met three sisters, the Misses Sylvia and Margaret Richardson and Mrs Kathleen Loe, who invited me to their cottage beside the river where Miss Hilda Green, a spritely eighty-year-old lady, joined us for tea. As we sat and watched the ducks come up from the river and the pheasants emerge from the undergrowth in the hope of picking up a few crumbs, we talked not of Constable but of A. J., a personal friend of the four ladies, and known to the rest of us as Sir Alfred James Munnings, K.C.V.O., Past President of the Royal Academy.

The ladies had first been introduced to the third of the Stour's great painters when he crossed the valley from his home at Castle House, Dedham, to visit their father, who then lived at Valley Farm, one of the oldest and smallest manor houses in Suffolk. In his autobiography, *The Finish,* A. J. recalled the happy scene at the ladies' childhood home, the roaring log fires in front of which their dog and cats warmed themselves in the company of a tame badger, nursed back to health by the girls after being injured, while a rook

looked down approvingly from a nearby cupboard. Munnings wrote, "Imagine a large living room with low black beamed ceiling. A wide open fireplace, half a tree trunk blazing and sparks flying up the chimney. The heat is glorious; so is the smell of lemons and punch which prevails in the dreamland scents of burning wood. Three sisters—sweet girls—the father, a widower—Leonard we call him, who likes good company . . ."

In return for their hospitality Alfred would bring along a bottle of port with a Stilton cheese and entertain the family until the early hours of the morning with songs and verse composed by himself. No doubt on this, as on every such occasion, he gave a fine rendering of his favourite song, *Julia*, which he composed himself.

Although Munnings' paternal grandfather lived and farmed in the Stour valley at Scotland Place, Stoke-by-Nayland, Alfred was born in 1878 and brought up in the Waveney valley at Mendham Mill, which was owned by his father. After attending school, first at Mendham and then at Framlingham College, which he hated, he became apprenticed to the Norwich firm of Page

Opposite: Castle House, Dedham, the home of Sir Alfred Munnings and now open to the public as a museum of the artist.

Right: A corner of Sir Alfred's studio at Castle House containing many of his favourite possessions. These pictures were taken by permission of Mr Stanley Booth, chairman of the Sir Alfred Munnings Art Museum.

Brothers, lithographers, as a poster artist and was soon designing chocolate and cracker box covers for the firm of Caley's, of Norwich. Some of this work is on display in his former studio in the grounds of Castle House, Dedham.

In his spare time he studied painting at the Norwich School of Art before going to Cornwall, where he was attracted by the Newlyn School. In 1898, the year his first picture *Stranded* was accepted by the Royal Academy, he lost the sight of his right eye when a thorn from a bramble pierced it as he lifted a puppy over a hedge. His injury caused him to be one of the first people to be subjected to X-rays.

This accident kept him out of the First World War, although he managed to spend the last year of it as a war artist attached to the Canadian Cavalry Brigade. His wartime work provided the evidence necessary for him to be elected as an Associate of the Royal Academy in 1919, the same year he purchased Castle House in Dedham. He resided there for the next forty years, except for a short spell when it was requisitioned by the army during the Second World War.

Munnings described Castle House as "The House of My Dreams", but it was probably the river and the surrounding valley that was the real attraction. "My one joy was knowing that my home was near a perfect river and a village in an unspoilt county."

Whilst he was often away from his home on painting assignments, he longed to be at home. "I long always to sit by a river and paint", he said, but he was not always satisfied with Castle House as his "painting spot", complaining that his studio was in the wrong place. "If I had bought the right place, I should have done great work" he once said. He also rented rooms at the old Grammar School in Dedham which he used as a studio.

It was to Castle House that Munnings brought his second bride, Violet McBride, herself an outstanding horsewoman who had won the Gold Cup at Olympia. Munnings' first marriage to Florence Carter-Wood in 1912 had ended in tragedy two years later when she poisoned herself with cyanide. Violet became his manager as well as his wife. No longer did the artist have to worry about such mundane matters as the management of money.

Sir Alfred is best remembered for his paintings of the equine and equestrian scene. Every situation which involved the life of a horse caught his attention; the gipsy encampments in the hop fields; the Royal processions at Ascot; the horse fairs at Lavenham and the racing scene; Newmarket was so close to his Dedham home. Portraiture earned him money, while he relaxed by painting in the open those landscapes he found so attractive by the River Stour.

He was elected President of the Royal Academy in 1944 and knighted by King George VI in the same year, and in 1946 he was made a Knight Commander of the Royal Victorian Order.

Many of Sir Alfred's paintings are on view to the public at Castle House. They have been tastefully hung in galleries which also house some of the family's exquisite furniture. One of the ladies I met at Flatford, Kathleen Loe, was the subject of Munnings' painting *The White Canoe,* which Munnings painted at Flatford.

At home in his valley, Sir Alfred was fascinated by and derived great pleasure from the small but intricate patterns created by nature. While out walking he would sit down to study the smallest detail of a daisy or examine some sheep's parsley, Queen Anne's Lace. On one occasion he phoned the editor of a national daily newspaper as he had something important to show him; it was the detailed pattern formed by the veins of a faded leaf!

He wrote to his wife, "When you want peace, paint willows and lily leaves." There is still an abundance of both by the Stour.

A. J. identified himself fully with the everyday life that went on around him in the Stour valley. He was a keen conservationist and deplored the degradation of the valley by tourists and modern methods of farming;

Pollarded willows beside the flooded Stour at Flatford. These used to provide poles and stakes for fencing and other purposes.

artificial fertiliser he referred to as "those bloody paper bags". He regretted the loss of sheep from the landscape, but while complaining that the land was not made to produce more food he objected to the production of sugar beet because it took goodness away from the land!

He fought hard for the preservation of the country scene he knew and loved, campaigning for the preservation of oak trees at Assington which were due to be felled. He paid out of his own pocket for the willows along the Stour to be pollarded, after obtaining the permission of the owner. At one time the willow tops were cut and used to make stakes, poles and hurdles, but when these became obsolete the trees were left to become top heavy so that the weight split the trunks apart. This negligence distressed Munnings.

He was instrumental in raising funds for the restoration of the famous cottages on the green at Cavendish and was disappointed when an appeal he launched to buy Gainsborough's house at Sudbury only reached a sum of £2,000, of which Munnings contributed £1,500 himself.

In the ruthless quest for his own high ideals he was outspoken, controversial, abrupt and sometimes rude. He also suffered badly from gout which on occasions sorely tried his patience. In his unprecedented Presidential speech at the Royal Academy banquet in 1949, which was broadcast to the nation, he left no one in any doubt as to his opinion of modern art and artists including Cézanne, Matisse and Picasso, to whom he referred as "foolish daubers", and gave a candid opinion of highbrows who presumed to be more knowledgeable than the painters.

If he could stir the emotions at a national level, he was equally adept locally. At a concert held in the Hewitt Hall, Dedham, to raise money to purchase a series of photographs of the village to send to their namesakes in America, Sir Alfred agreed to give his rendering of *Julia*. Percy Edwards, the well-known bird impressionist, also gave of his talents.

All went well until the end of the performance when the chairman of the Parish Council announced that his council was attempting to have the local bus service improved. This immediately prompted Sir Alfred to go on to the stage and launch in public a bitter attack on the chairman for not having maintained the footpath between Dedham and Flatford properly. He even offered to pay the cost of repair from his own pocket. Such was the character of this artist who had won international acclaim in his own lifetime but had found his own "Moment of Arcadia" here in the meadows beside the Stour.

"I was in the meadow adjoining the river and on the sloping bank I lay down," he wrote. "Happier by far than I have been these twenty years. The reason being that I had sought and found the spot I must find at the moment or die. So satisfying were my surroundings that it is impossible to express my feelings. I could only sigh and groan with pleasure. Downstream I could see the roofs and chimneys of Stoke-by-Nayland through the trees. Behind me a row of willows and a poplar tree which rustled crisply, making its own separate sound."

Sir Alfred Munnings died on 17th July, 1959, and a memorial tablet was placed in his memory next to that of John Constable in St Paul's Cathedral.

Constable's Flatford Mill is now world-famous and Willy Lott's cottage next door is the best-known domicile in England. During the sixteenth century the mill was used for fulling cloth, in Constable's time for milling corn, and it is now used by the Field Studies Council, who run residential courses here for students of all ages in such far-ranging subjects as ecology, ornithology, natural history and, of course, painting. Willy Lott's cottage is used to accommodate the students.

Opposite: Flatford mill, East Bergholt, which was owned by Golding Constable, father of John Constable.

Right: Willy Lott's cottage beside the Stour just below Flatford mill.

Little is known of Willy except that he was a delicate child and was unable to go away to school. He lived, however, for eighty-eight years and, it is said, never left his home for more than a few hours during this time—who could blame him?

Crossing the Stour by the quaint wooden-arched Flatford footbridge, it is a pleasant walk past the mill to Judas Gap where a branch of the river meets an extended arm of the tidal estuary. A weir at this point stops the sea reaching Flatford. The path continues along the bank of this salt river until it reaches the Cattawade barrage alongside the A137. The alternative path from Flatford, which is not so easy, follows roughly the old navigation channel to Brantham Lock and Cattawade bridge.

A new barrage on the seaward side of Cattawade bridge prevents the tide coming up the river to Flatford Lock, and this stretch of the river has reverted to fresh water. At Brantham the horses were unharnessed from the barges and left to graze in the adjacent meadows to await their next session of travail, while the barges crossed the estuary to Mistley by wind or manpower.

The great-great-grandson of Willy Lott's brother John, describing this part of the river to the Stour Antiquarian Society in 1969, said, "My favourite spot for a swim, after a day's work in the city, was just above Brantham Lock. In winter I always carried a hurricane lantern to inspect the water surface for floating debris before diving in. I remember watching otters playing near Brantham mill." This was at the beginning of this century.

The fields on the hill above the lock were the first in East Anglia to be sown with barley. Thomas Tusser, who lived at Braham Hall, not the present building but its predecessor, was the farmer who sowed the seed during the sixteenth century and recorded the event in his book, *A Hundred Pointes of Good Husbandrie*. He later expanded the points to five hundred.

Between Brantham Lock and the tidal estuary stands a little eighteenth-century hump-backed bridge which has a character all of its own. It has now been made redundant by a modern bridge which carries the main road across the river, leaving the old bridge free for children to play and fish. On a bright, calm, sunny summer's day large carp, mainly Mirror carp with the occasional Common carp, can be seen basking in the fresh water around the base of the bridge. As dusk approaches they move out into the river in search of food, a task which continues throughout the night unless there is a sudden drop in temperature or a marked change in the atmospheric pressure. In the early morning, these monsters among fish can be seen leaping from the water, re-entering it tail first before returning to the shade of the bridge.

This is a good place to fish. Between the new bridge and the sluice fishing is free, apart from the Essex area A.W.A. rod licence. There is plenty of

Roger Clark, of Weylands Farm, Stoke-by-Nayland, shoeing a horse at Barrett's Farm, Dedham, next door to the home of Sir Alfred Munnings.

roach, gudgeon and pike all the year round, to which can be added the carp, a few tench and plenty of eels during the summer. Winter is the best time for bream and chub, as they tend to move upstream during the summer.*

During the reign of Henry VIII Robert Debnam was hanged on Cattaway Causeway. His crime, along with three others, was to burn the crucifix which stood above the rood screen in All Saints' church, Dovercourt. Miraculous powers were attributed to this crucifix and the church grew rich on the takings from gullible pilgrims, a fact which grieved the Protestant reformers. Four of them broke into the church, stole the cruficix and burnt it on Dovercourt Green in 1532. Three were caught and hanged, the fourth, Robert Gardener, lived to tell the tale, which was recorded in Foxe's *Book of Martyrs.*

A century later in 1648 Cattawade Bridge reverberated to the hoofs of Parliamentary cavalry under Lord Fairfax as they gave chase to a party of Royalist cavalry sent out by Sir Charles Lucas to search for food for the besieged garrison at Colchester. Meanwhile frigates of the Navy loyal to Cromwell stood off Harwich ready to assist that town if the Royalists broke out from Colchester and attacked the port.

Daniel Defoe on his journey through the counties of Eastern England in 1724 records sending his horses by way of Cattawade Bridge while he took a boat up the Orwell, to meet them at Ipswich. "I sent my horses round by Manningtree, where there is a timber bridge over the Stour, called Cataway Bridge," he wrote. It could not have been long after this that the wooden bridge was replaced by the present brick structure.

Beyond the bridge on the Suffolk side of the estuary stands the plastics factory, still known locally as BX though it now displays the name of Storeys. The older and taller buildings in this complex detract sadly from the open views along the estuary, and several attempts to cultivate trees as a screen have failed because of the salt in the soil by the river's edge. The site is, however, important to the local economy and has a fascinating history going back a hundred years to the pioneering attempts to find substitutes for ivory, tortoise-shell and gutta-percha.

The factory had its beginning at Hackney in the East End of London. Alexander Parkes had made a brown material from nitro-cellulose which he called Parkesine and exhibited it at the Great Exhibition in South Kensington in 1862. Parkes also discovered how to waterproof material and sold the patents to Charles MacIntosh, who gave his name to the Mackintosh raincoat.

Daniell Spill noticed the material at the exhibition and in 1864 started to manufacture it at his factory in Hackney, where he had been making water-proof cloth. Two years later Parkes and Spill floated the Parkesine Company, but Spill was to acquire all the assets and set up his own company, the Xylonite Co. Ltd. Xylonite comes from the Greek meaning wood, and the artificial product obtained from nitro-cellulose was called Xyloidine. He purchased two

*I am indebted to Nigel Baker for the information on fishing.

Mr Leslie Mills with his pair of Shire horses waiting to enter the ring at the Suffolk Show. His "heavy horse centre" at Dedham is popular with visitors.

houses in Homerton High Street, Hackney, in which he manufactured a white plastic material used for making knife handles and a plastic paste to insulate electric cables. The product made by mixing nitro-cellulose with camphor and vegetable oil was not a success and the company was wound up in 1872.

Meanwhile, in America, John Wesley Hyatt had made a better product by using a greater proportion of camphor in the mix. His product was celluloid, and his was the first real achievement in making a suitable plastic material. In 1876 the new American process was brought to the attention of Levi Parsons Merriam, who set up a small factory in an adjacent house to Spill and manufactured imitation coral jewellery from the Xylonite he obtained from next door. The following year, 1877, Spill's factory and the Merriam business combined to form the British Xylonite Co. Limited and BX was born, their main product being combs which replaced the jewellery. By 1884 they had extended the range of their products to include imitation ivory for combs and keyboards, but more important products were plastic shirt fronts, collars and cuffs which did not require laundering.

It was probably the increased business from the sale of collars and cuffs which was responsible for bringing the BX factory to the Stour valley. The bigger work force operating in very cramped conditions at Hackney together with the high fire risk in a residential district necessitated a search for new premises.

The hundred-and-thirty acre site of Brooklands Farm near Cattawade Bridge was chosen. The land being marshy and liable to flooding was cheap, £30 an acre, but the site possessed good communications with London by sea and by rail. A decision to purchase was made in April, 1887, and by the October the factory was in operation. Fifty-six cottages were built on the hill overlooking the river to house the workers from London, while the factory was built on the low-lying ground on both sides of the railway. Many of the cottages are still to be seen adjacent to the factory in New Village, so called to distinguish it from the main village of Brantham further up the hill.

Claude Paget, the factory manager, resided at Crowe Hall along the river at Stutton. It is said that he rode to work each day on horseback, his horse shod

Canoeists receive final instructions in front of the old Cattawade Bridge before navigating the Stour.

with shoes made from Xylonite. The local boys followed him to work at a safe distance, hoping to see the plastic shoes ignite.

The celluloid made at Brantham can be sliced either into thin sheets from which table tennis balls are made or into thick sheets used to make dice; the clear transparent colours make it possible to ensure that they have not been loaded. Substantial quantities go for export, many to Las Vegas.

Poly Vinyl Chloride (PVC) forms the basis of the modern plastics factory at Brantham. PVC powder is mixed with plasticiser oils and colourants, then kneaded into a dough to be formed into a continuous sheet by passing it through a series of heated rollers. It can then be embossed to give the grained appearance of wood or leather. Used as a surface laminate with chipboard or hardboard, the durable and decorative sheets are used for furniture and television cabinets while steel laminate is used in the construction industry. Colchester's multi-storey car park at the central bus station has exterior cladding of steel/PVC laminate panels.

Plastic beer hoses through which the beer flows from the barrel to the glass are also made from PVC, and until recently the firm employed a dedicated band of tasters to ensure that no taint of plastic could be detected in the beer.

Next door the firm of Hercules operates a plant making a thin clear plastic wrapping material from polypropylene for wrapping biscuits and other things.

The production of thin cellulose sheet for photographic film base was started at Brantham in 1932. After the Second World War the film plant became jointly owned by BX and Ilford, taking the name Bexford, and it was taken over by I.C.I. in 1970 and now produces the film base from terylene and other materials.

The way along the Stour continues from the Brantham works over Cattawade Bridge to join the main road for a short distance until it crosses the salt river to meet the other path coming from Flatford mill on the Essex side of the new barrage. At the top of the hill in Lawford is Lawford Place, used by BX as a research establishment for a time. Mrs Margaret Thatcher, the first woman Prime Minister, worked here as a research chemist.

Lawford Hall, an Elizabethan house built in 1583 and given a Georgian facade in 1756, stands at the bottom of the hill near the station. It was built on the site of a former hall which together with property at East Bergholt formed part of King Harold's manor. It passed to William the Conqueror after 1066, remaining a Royal possession through the reigns of Henry VI, Henry VIII, Edward VI and Mary, although it was rarely, if ever visited by them.

Returning to the footpath, one now passes along the Essex bank under the railway and having passed the industrial environs, has one's first view of the Stour estuary. The walk finishes behind the *Skinner's Arms* in Manningtree.

CHAPTER EIGHT

The Stour Estuary

THE twenty-two acres of Manningtree, the place of many trees, wedged between Lawford and Mistley, is the smallest parish in Essex. Travellers to Europe will recognise its station, a mile to the west of the town on the main London line and in the parish of Lawford, as the rail junction for Harwich and the Continent. Underneath a British Rail sign which reads "Manningtree for the Continent" some humourist has written "and Colchester for the Incontinent."

Before the railway reached Manningtree in 1846 it was, along with Mistley, a thriving bustling port. For a time it benefited from deep-water fishing vessels which came up the river to off-load their catches directly on to the trains for London instead of mooring at Harwich. The railway reached Harwich in 1854, and after this date Manningtree went into a decline. Not only did the railway take the trade away from the river but the local craftsmen who made and sold shoes, clothing, furniture and other household commodities now had to compete with manufactured goods brought in by rail.

The present high cost of petrol, the difficulty and expense of parking cars and the traffic congestion in the larger towns of Colchester and Ipswich has created an economic revival in Manningtree and other similar small market towns. New shops have now opened within its historic buildings, which together with the open-air Saturday market provide the customer with leisurely shopping in a town where car parking is free.

The charm and character of Manningtree is enhanced by the variety of its ancient buildings. The Dutch weavers' cottages at the top of the hill in South Street vie with the Old Coffee House as to which is the oldest building, while the Dutch influence can be seen in the Mansard roofs. These are a steep sloping roof which supports another of lesser angle.

The Old Coffee House, now completely restored by Essex County Council, stands near the Old Quay and was probably built some time during the sixteenth century. The original purpose of the building is not clear. It could have been a Guildhall, a toll house or a lock-up; until recently the recessed walls in the cellar had chains hanging on them. During the eighteenth century it became a coffee house, and like the famous Lloyds' coffee house in London, from which grew the present Lloyds' of London, underwriters, the Manningtree shop would have been the place where merchants conducted their business.

Later stronger liquor was brewed on the premises, and some of the copper vessels used in the process have been discovered. At the beginning of the twentieth century the shop was owned by a Mr Downing, a clockmaker and ironmonger. Since its restoration, in which it gained a splendid mock-Tudor front, it has been used as an antique shop, and it is now a restaurant in which one can dine with elegance beneath its sixteenth-century oak beams.

It is, however, Georgian architecture which predominates in Manningtree's main streets. Built of brick, the houses, or as is frequently the case the house fronts, are easily recognised by the symmetrically placed rectangular windows and the central doorways, elaborately decorated in Classical style. For the first time, chimneys were placed at the ends of the house, so that inside the central fireplaces give way to magnificent staircases.

Soft wood from Scandinavia was used to make the windows and doors and this, unlike the English oak, had to be protected from the weather by using white lead paint. This gave the Georgian houses their other characteristic feature, white paintwork. Not everybody could afford new houses in the Georgian style, so many timber-framed buildings were modernised by constructing a Georgian front to cover the Tudor timber frame, an economical way of keeping up with the Joneses. The most impressive Georgian houses, once the homes of the wealthy Manningtree merchants, are to be found at the top of

Georgian shop fronts in Manningtree High Street.

South Street. The largest of them all is No. 50 in the High Street, which has a splendid Doric doorway.

Any thriving seaport, especially if it is backed by an agrarian population, demands a good supply of ale for its sustenance. The neighbouring parish of Mistley is still the centre of an important malting industry and between them the two parishes could boast of no fewer than eighteen public houses in 1882. Like the coffee houses, much business was conducted on these premises, which also acted as labour exchanges where labourers and servants could be hired, while the more important inns were sometimes used as courts.

Of the two coaching inns, the *White Hart* and the *Packet*, only the former remains as an inn, the latter now being Townsend's stationery shop in the town centre. The *White Hart*, surmounted by a figure of this animal, takes its name from the emblem of Richard II, but dates from the sixteenth century and was refaced with brick two hundred years later. From here the Harwich coach, the Defiance, departed daily for London; Winter's waggon left twice a week for Long Melford.

The *Packet*, whose buildings date from the fifteenth century, backed on to the Manningtree quayside and was an inn from 1737 until 1914, when it became a labour exchange for a while before being purchased by Townsend's in 1955 and opened as a stationer's shop in 1960. It must have been a large and

The team from the Crown relax after competing in the tug o'war at Manningtree Regatta, an event which entails the competitors getting well covered in mud.

important establishment, as Petty Sessions were held here and it had stabling for 200 horses. The market and annual fair were held outside its premises and market stalls were erected in the inn yard. Stage coaches left from here at five in the morning every day the fare being 15/6 (77½p) if you sat in the coach or 7/6 (37½p) if you travelled on the outside. Manningtree High Street must have presented a very colourful scene as the ostlers prepared the horses and loaded the coaches in preparation for a long, hazardous and uncomfortable journey to London. The early morning commuter who now catches the train for London and accomplishes the journey in just over an hour may feel that times have not changed very much as he fights for a seat on the 7.10 a.m.

The *Crown*, previously known as the *Rose and Crown*, stands on the eastern edge of the town and has its inn yard running down to the river. From here carriers operated a hundred years ago taking goods to Colchester and Ipswich two or three times a week. Adjacent to the inn yard is the clubhouse of the Manningtree Sailing Club. During the club's annual regatta the *Crown* challenges the club to a tug-of-war in the mud on the Manningtree shore, teams of men and women donning fancy dress for the occasion. Father Neptune presides over the event, which becomes a fight for survival as the contestants, wallowing in the black, thick, sticky, mud up to their thighs, cling firmly to the rope to prevent themselves being engulfed. Races across the muddy shore also take place, the competitors strapping boards to their feet to prevent them sinking. It is a hilarious event and attracts large crowds.

From Manningtree the road, known as the Strand, follows the river closely along the border of what was once the extravagantly ornate gardens of Mistley Hall, the home of the Rigby family. An ornamental lake and a small but distinguished white stone bridge, which carries the Strand over a rivulet trickling out of the lake, are reminders of more glorious days. Here on bright, sunny Sunday afternoons family motorists park their cars to purchase ice creams for their children and to feed the swans.

There are more than 600 swans on this part of the river, representing the second largest swannery in England. It is believed that they have been attracted here by the waste from the old maltings, but now that these have become obsolete and are being pulled down, it is feared that the swan population may decrease.

At the end of the Strand stands Mistley towers, looking rather forlorn and out of place. They are two square stone towers crowned with circular domes, embellished with Tuscan columns, and are all that remains of Mistley Thorn Church, built in 1735. This plain red-brick church was given a facelift in 1777 by Robert Adam to give it tone and to harmonise it with the rest of the Rigby estate by building the neo-classical towers on to each end of the church and adding a portico with Tuscan columns. It was the only ecclesiastical work executed by Robert and was quite unlike any other English church. Unfortunately it was demolished in 1870. The Tuscan columns were transferred to the towers to give them symmetry, and these were left standing as navigational aids for craft on the river.

Edward Rigby was a London linen draper who had purchased an interest in the Earl of Oxford's estate. On the death of the Earl in 1703 there was a dispute over his affairs which was settled by an Act of Parliament giving Edward Rigby possession of the Mistley estates, which passed to his son, Richard. The latter sold the linen business and, having made a fortune out of the South Sea Company, came to live at Mistley, where he built himself Mistley Hall and a new town for his tenants. He constructed a new quay, a dock large enough to accommodate two vessels and warehouses, granaries and maltings. When Rigby died in 1730 he left in his will £300 for the construction of almshouses which were to be maintained out of the dock profits.

Richard Rigby's son, also Richard, was only eight when his father died. He had received little formal education but at the age of twenty-one completed the Grand Tour of Europe before embarking on a notorious political career. Richard became Member of Parliament for Castle Rising in 1745, and two years later M.P. for Sudbury. In 1754 his association with the Duke of Bedford gave him the seat at Tavistock, and when the Duke became Lord Lieutenant of Ireland in 1758 he made Rigby his secretary and

spokesman in the Irish Parliament. George III made him the Paymaster of the Forces in 1768, a lucrative post as he was able to lend out government money and pocket the interest. He is believed to have made half a million pounds. Not surprisingly Rigby opposed any legislation which sought to restrict influence by bribery.

He was flamboyant, fashionable, self-indulgent, extravagant and corrupt. He had a weakness for the ladies, and it is recorded that he left £5,000 to an illegitimate daughter and £1,000 to her mother. He entertained lavishly at Mistley Hall, which was conveniently situated for his friends who travelled from London to the Continent through Harwich. His guests included Horace Walpole, Garrick and Frederick, Prince of Wales, who at one stage promised Rigby the Lordship of the Bedchamber but then changed his mind.

It was Rigby's intention to make Mistley into a spa town rather like Bath. Although he retired to Bath and died there in 1788 he was buried in the family vault at Mistley. He had plans to build a saltwater bath near the river, but it was never completed, although the spa pavilion still stands behind the swan fountain in the square. Mistley Hall was rebuilt in lavish style and the gardens landscaped with oriental temples and bridges, the church was given its Classical facade and the 700 acres of his estate, which spread into thirteen parishes and included eight or nine manors, was planted with avenues of

Right: Mistley Towers, all that remain of the old church, demolished in 1870.

Opposite: Swans on the Strand between Manningtree and Mistley.

exotic trees and shrubs, many of which still survive. It must have been a magnificent place in a beautiful setting, with the harbour filled with sailing ships and barges, behind which stood the bright new buildings dotted among the tree-covered slopes rising gently from the river. A Frenchman, François de la Rochefoucauld, visited Mistley in 1784 and gave this description in his journal, printed in this century as *A Frenchman in England:*

> "Mistley is a very pretty place consisting of rather more than 50 houses, which are so neat and well built, that it is obvious at a glance that they all belong to one man. Mr Rigby owns the whole town—the Inn also belongs to Mr Rigby . . . The Harbour is faced with a high brick wall to which the whalers are fixed. At the end of it there is quite a large warehouse where merchants put all they want without paying. At the end of the harbour there is a small shipbuilding yard in which I saw two forty-tonners under construction. The trade of the place is wholly created by Mr Rigby. It consists of coal and iron imported from other parts of England and four or five vessels are employed in the work of transport. Near the port there is a lime-kiln which has been faced with brick and made into the shape of a fort.
>
> "Mistley Hall is of white brick. The drawing rooms and dining rooms are magnificent. The furniture in the bedrooms is simple but fine and the gardens the best I have seen in England. The lawn is mown weekly; there are rare trees, a curved gravel drive, two tulip trees 60-80ft in circumference. This is in the garden which is surrounded by a ha-ha.* Beyond it is a succession of gardens for two miles. There are fine cows on the Hall's farm—hares, pheasants, deer; nine acres of kitchen garden with fruit trees from France; large hot houses with peaches, pineapples and cherries."

On Rigby's death the estate passed to his nephew, Colonel Francis Hale Rigby, and he in turn left it to his daughter Frances, the wife of Lord Rivers, who was accidently drowned in the Serpentine. By now the place was becoming neglected. In 1834 Mistley Hall became the home of the Rt. Hon. Charles Manners Sutton, Speaker of the House of Commons. Ten years later the estate was sold and the Hall demolished. Today all that remains of this splendid place are the stables and the Adams lodges which stood at the entrances.

Malting is Mistley's oldest industry, having its roots back in the seventeenth century. Within a hundred years the maltsters had become the most influential businessmen in the town, by 1841 controlling no fewer than seventeen maltings, much to the dismay of the local temperance society. The rapid expansion of the malting industry was undoubtedly due to the building by Richard Rigby in 1739 of Mistley quay, from which malt was sent daily by

*Ha-ha—sunken fence.

barge to the London breweries. The finest English barley was, and still is, grown in East Anglia and used to be brought to Mistley by barge and horse-drawn waggon. Chubb Horlock, Mistley's famous barge skipper, recalls that it was not unusual to see a queue of waggons a quarter of a mile long waiting to discharge grain at the quayside granary.

In 1810 Edward Norman built new maltings and employed a William Brooks from Little Bentley. Brooks's son became the manager of the company, and when the owner died in 1862 the business was left to him. The Brooks name plate is still prominent on some of the buildings, although by 1870 he was facing keen competition from Messrs Free, Rodwell and Company, who

Where barges were once built at Mistley there is now a small shipbreaking yard. The trawler on the right once voyaged to northern waters in search of cod.

built between 1870 and 1902 what were believed to be the best set of maltings in England. Malt from this firm was sent directly to Dublin to Guinness' brewery.

EDME, The English Diastatic Malt Extract Company was established in 1881 as an offshoot of Free, Rodwell's and they are at present the largest producers of malt and malt extract in the United Kingdom. When in 1963 the Chancellor of the Exchequer repealed the Act of Parliament which made it necessary to have a licence before alcoholic beverages could be brewed at home, EDME were inundated with requests from keen amateur home brewers for small quantities of their malt products. So great was the demand that the firm decided to produce carefully prepared home-brew kits from which the amateur would have little difficulty in obtaining an excellent product.

EDME produce about 7,000 tons of malt and malt extract in a year, about 1,500 tons of which, sufficient for four million pints, goes into home-brew kits, while a similar quantity goes to the professional breweries. The remainder, nearly 50%, is used in the confectionery trade to make malt drinks, chocolates and breakfast foods. Being a keen amateur brewer myself, I visited EDME's factory in the hope of gaining a few useful tips on improving my own brew. I was met by Bob Pritchard, the sales director, himself a keen home brewer, and shown around their modern factory by Brian Hill, their production director.

Malt is made by soaking barley grain in water for about three days, during which time it absorbs about half its own weight of moisture. In the traditional maltings, the barley was then spread thinly on the malting floors and turned with wooden shovels while the grain germinated and sprouted a shoot. After about a week, during which time the grain was gradually transferred from the ground floor to the upper storeys, the green malt was transferred to the kiln where it was dried. During the germination process important enzymes known collectively as Diastase are formed within the barley, hence the word Diastatic in the company name.

After drying, the malt, looking very much the same as the barley from which it was made, is screened to remove the culm* and then stored for several weeks before being used. The process has now been modernised, the germination and drying processes now taking place in rotating drums, which require less manpower and make it possible to automate the process. This has resulted in the rapid demolition of the traditional maltings at both Manningtree and Mistley. The kilns with their characteristic pyramid-shaped roofs topped by the kiln louvre, which have been a familiar landmark for so long, will soon be no more.

Malt extract, that thick, sticky brown liquid, is manufactured by steeping the malt in hot water to make a mash in which the diastase converts the starch, originally stored in the barley seed, into fermentable sugars. It is not possible to

*Culm — the dried shoots, sold for animal food.

Morris dancers exhibit their age-old traditions at Manningtree.

change starch directly into alcohol, hence the necessity for the malting process. The mash is then evaporated to produce the sticky malt extract, often referred to wrongly as "malt". In a brewery a similar mash is strained to produce the wort, fermented into beer by adding yeast, together with hops for flavour. The yeast works on the sugars in the malt to convert it to alcohol (ethanol) and carbon dioxide. Although more sugar can be added to make the beer extra strong, Bob Pritchard advised against it as it can ruin the flavour and spoil the head. The best commercial beers, he told me, are made from malt and hops only.

Other advice he had for the home brewer included

(i) paying particular attention to cleanliness. All apparatus should be washed with a sterilising detergent before rinsing it in a sterilising solution of sodium metabisulphite.

(ii) Make sure the brew doesn't come into contact with the air, otherwise you might get vinegar instead.

(iii) Temperature of the brew is critical and should be between 65-80 degrees Fahrenheit.

(iv) Only add one teaspoonful of priming sugar to each pint bottle. This adds sparkle to the beer but add too much in the hope of producing more alcohol and the bottle will probably blow up.

(v) Beer doesn't improve with keeping. It is in the peak of condition after it has been bottled for about a month, so don't be a martyr, drink up and enjoy it.

The *Thorn Inn* stands opposite Mistley quay in a small square containing a fountain, appropriately in the form of a swan, which was to have been the centre of Rigby's spa town. It has been providing strong, clear, English ale to generations of its customers, coach travellers and lumpers, the name given to the quay workers, alike for more than two hundred years. For most of the time laughter and gaiety spilled out from the *Thorn* to liven the square with the help of buskers who performed outside to earn a few coppers, but this was not always so. During the middle of the seventeenth century, at the time of the English Civil War, it was the headquarters of Matthew Hopkins, the notorious self-styled Witch Finder General.

In this period the *Thorn* must have resembled a Gestapo headquarters where people, particularly women, were taken to be interrogated and charged with witchcraft. If the methods of making them talk were less sophisticated than they are today, they must have been more effective, because although spies and enemy agents do exist, witches never did. Undoubtedly during this time of hatred, particularly between the Parliamentarians and the Royalists, Hopkins, for the appropriate fee, was able to dispose of enemies from both sides under the guise of witchcraft. Otherwise it is difficult to see how he grew so rich, as the fee was only twenty shillings for a successful prosecution. King

The courtyard of the *Thorn Inn* at Mistley. Is that the ghost of Matthew Hopkins skulking under the archway?

James I was fascinated by witchcraft and in 1597 published three books entitled *Daemonologie* which laid down the ground rules for witch-hunting, and new laws were passed based on their contents.

To accuse a person of witchcraft successfully it was necessary to show that she had been associating with the devil, usually by sleeping with him, when he would leave behind bites and other scars about her body.* Any carbuncles, piles or warts, particularly about the private parts, provided good evidence, and then it was a simple matter to obtain a confession by denying the victim any food or sleep. Marks left by the devil would not bleed when pricked, so it was believed. Pricking scars to see if they bled was of course performed by a man; Scotland had a team of professional prickers, who resorted to all sorts of tricks including the use of retractable pins to ensure that bleeding would not take place and that a conviction would result.

If a suspect was devoid of any scars, pimples or nodules the ancient Teutonic custom of trial by "swimming" was certain to produce the required evidence. It was believed that the pure element water, not an element and rarely pure, would not allow a guilty person to drown in it. The unfortunate person was stripped and then clothed in a loose fitting smock, having had the big toes tied to the opposite thumbs. The victim was then lowered three times into a pool of water by a rope tied round the waist. If she drowned, a verdict of not guilty was pronounced, but survival meant guilt and the lady was convicted and hanged. A system used as early as 2,000 B.C. to detect murderers and adulterers.

It is not certain how Matthew Hopkins became interested in his grisly career or how he met his end. He was born the son of a vicar, the Reverend James Hopkins, of Great Wenham in Suffolk. He visited the Netherlands during his youth and may have received part of his education there, and he might have witnessed the persecution of the Huguenots. Hopkins started work as a solicitor's clerk in Ipswich before moving to a shipping office in Mistley. Although he may have started hunting witches at first for financial reasons, he soon became flushed with his success and obsessed by power, and before long he was a fanatic. He came to believe that he had been divinely appointed to his task and that he was in possession of the Devil's list of English witches.

Fortunately his reign of terror lasted for only three years, from 1644 to 1647, the first year being the most active of his campaign. We know how his reign of terror began, Elizabeth Clarke, an eighty-year-old lady with only one leg, being his first victim, but the end of the story is not known with certainty. The burial of a Matthew Hopkings, son of the Minister of Wenham, is recorded at Mistley Church as taking place on 12th August, 1647. It is believed he might have been treated to a dose of his own medicine, trial by drowning or swimming, in Mistley pool, conviction and execution. Others say he died of consumption whilst hiding from the mob in a friend's house.

*Scars in England were more often attributed to bites from the witch's imps, usually her family pets.

In 1692 witch trials were inaugurated in Massachusetts, New England, on similar lines to those held in Mistley. This has led to the suggestion that Hopkins escaped to America to join his brother and continue his macabre activities. However Hopkins' ghost has been seen in Mistley on too many occasions for this to be true. It haunts the local pubs and the church and has been seen most frequently along the sea wall, particularly near Hopping bridge, the bridge on the Strand, where some believe him to have been buried. "The grass is greener there," one local comic informed me over a glass of beer when I asked how he knew the body was buried there. The bridge was built about a hundred years after Hopkins' time.

The Hopkins apparition was last seen, it must be ten years ago now, by a young lady, Janice Golding, who came face to face with the ghost in the attic of the *Thorn Inn*. I understand that she departed rather hastily. I had a curious experience when I visited the *Thorn* one Christmas recently to take pictures of it for this book and to talk to Pat Smith, the landlady, about the ghost. Having taken pictures of the attic where the ghost appeared I was attracted to the courtyard, which had something of a Dickensian atmosphere about it. Thinking it would make a pleasant Christmas picture I asked if I could return that evening and take pictures using a flashgun to obtain the effect of a cold winter's evening, with the light from the inn's windows lighting the courtyard to give a warm homely effect.

At least that was the idea. I completed the assignment about 4 o'clock that afternoon and returned home and processed the film. Astonishingly, on one negative was the outline of a person standing in the corner of the courtyard. Next day, being a Saturday, I returned to the inn to show the pictures to the landlord and customers, who as they entered the bar divided themselves into two camps, those who thought it was Hopkins and the others who thought it was a trick. So hot did the discussion become that, believing that discretion really is the better part of valour, I slipped away unnoticed. I think myself that some trick of light and a series of coincidences had been responsible for the uncanny image.

However, I phoned the *Thorn Inn* as I was writing this to ask if there has been any more recent manifestations at the inn. It was under new management and the new landlady, being unaware of my picture, informed me that nothing untoward had happened at the *Thorn*, that she was aware of the existence of the ghost and that a few weeks ago she took some pictures of her husband in the courtyard. When they were processed they noticed a hand apparently patting her husband on the head.

From Mistley the country road twists its tortuous way to Harwich, giving fine views of the Stour estuary. A mile out of Mistley is Bradfield, the home of Sir Harbottle Grimston, who was born here in 1603, became Member of Parliament for Harwich and Colchester, and in 1660 as Speaker of the House of Commons greeted Charles II on his arrival at Dover to reclaim the crown of England.

At Ramsey the road joins the main road from Colchester, which follows the last of the Stour tributaries, the Ramsey Brook, from Wix Green through to Parkeston, where it enters the Stour. The journey to Parkeston and Harwich, at the mouth of the river, is more interesting and spectacularly beautiful if it is undertaken by boat with the tide full on a warm summer's day. I sailed with fisherman Peter Page, who has been working these waters in practically every moment of his spare time since he was ten years old. Extensive mud flats cover the estuary, and an accurate knowledge of the position of the deep water channels, the main one running along the Essex side of the river, together with an understanding of the tides and the weather are necessary to sail these waters, which can be very treacherous. More than one amateur sailor has been stranded on the mud overnight by a receding tide.

Besides setting his eel traps in the gullies, Peter catches a lot of mullet, which feed off the mud banks during the summer months. When he sees the

Peter Page returning after a day's fishing on the Stour estuary.

The Tudor gateway of Stutton Hall.

fish leaping from the water, he anchors his boat, a lifeboat which he converted himself to a fishing smack, and rows round the shoal in his dinghy paying out the net as he goes. The encircled fish have no escape as he draws the net tighter around them. Mullet are becoming a popular edible fish, to replace cod and plaice which are increasingly scarce and costly on the open market.

Our boat headed out from Mistley towards the northern or Suffolk shore and Stutton Hall. The original Hall, which goes back to the time of Henry VIII or even Henry VII, is enclosed by a brick boundary wall with a curious gateway similar in style to the gatehouse to Erwarton Hall but smaller, mainly Gothic in character with a stepped gable on the outside and a semi-circular pediment inside placed between four tall pinnacles. The buildings were probably constructed from brick made from the local brickearth found in Stutton. The Hall, with its fine spiralling ornamental Tudor chimneys, is a fine example from that period of history.

Next door, or rather a few fields away downstream, stands Crowe Hall, another remarkable building of similar date to Stutton Hall. Its great bedchamber has a very rich and elaborately moulded plaster ceiling, believed to have been done by the same craftsman that executed the very finely detailed plasterwork on Sparrowe's House in the Buttermarket at Ipswich, now the Ancient House bookshop. During the nineteenth century Crowe Hall underwent a transformation in the Gothic style and its battlements and turret overlooking one of the most picturesque parts of the estuary bring to mind a Scottish Highland castle.

Having left Stutton Point to port, we dropped anchor off Wrabness at the widest part of the estuary, two miles across. The Harwich cod fishermen used to come up here to catch dabs and also whelks with which to bait their cod-lines. Dabs and whelks were caught by using a net stretched over a hoop, baited with crab meat and lowered to the river bed where the whelks crawled into the hoops and were then raised to the surface.

A dredger near us deliberately and unhurriedly worked its way upstream excavating gravel from the river bed to be loaded into barges, which were towed upstream to Mistley, where the gravel is unloaded for use in the building industry. For many years Manningtree builders floated their lighters downstream to beach them at low tide on Ballast Hill, where they would shovel the shingle on board or scoop it up using a leather bucket with holes in it attached to a wire rim, known as a doydle.

We had anchored off Wrabness to watch the Thames sailing barges make their way upriver during the annual Pin Mill sailing race, which takes place in July each year. The barges start from Butterman's Bay on the Orwell, where the larger sailing ships once dropped anchor to unload their cargoes of grain

A flycatcher made its nest in a wayside shrine of St Christopher and the Christ child at Stutton for several years running.

into the barges. They race past Harwich, turn to come up the Stour as far as Wrabness, and then return downstream to Bloody Point, where they return to the Orwell and finish at Pin Mill.

The steamer *Puffin*, the pride and joy of its skipper Bob Partis, came out of Holbrook creek with a party of spectators to join us at our anchorage. Bob is fanatical about steam engines and treats his boat, a full-time hobby, to the fondest of care and attention. What is it about steam, I often wonder, which is so fascinating, when petrol, diesel and electric propulsion hardly turn the head? The *Puffin* was one of His Majesty's Harbour Service Launches, built towards the end of the First World War. She is the only one remaining from this period. Her steam engine consumes a hundredweight of fuel (56 kilos) an hour to propel the craft at a speed of eight knots. With a displacement of 36 tons *Puffin* is made of teak, apart from the wheel house and floorboards, which had to be replaced after two seamen took her from Scapa Flow to the Shetlands but missed the islands and found themselves heading into the Atlantic and running out of coal. They chopped up part of the boat to use as fuel to get them back to St Ninian's Isle (Shetland).

A small steam tug was used on the Stour at the turn of the century to tow rafts of logs round from Ipswich to the sawmill at Manningtree and also to pull barges upstream.

The Thames sailing barges have always been raced by their skippers either for pleasure or to be first home with the cargo. It was Henry Dodd who in 1863 first introduced the annual sailing races on the Thames to encourage improvements in barge design and to promote better seamanship. Dodd made a fortune using his barge to take London's rubbish downriver to the dumps. As the *Thalatta*, a barge used to give schoolchildren educational adventure cruises along the coast, rounded the buoy, we slipped our anchor, took a look back at the impressive buildings of the Royal Hospital School on the north bank and followed the procession of barges to Parkeston Quay. The barges with their red ochre spritsails are still one of the finest and most exciting sights around our coast.

Parkeston Quay is the ferry passenger terminal for the North Sea ferry services. It was built by the Great Eastern Railway on Ray Island, two miles up the Stour from Harwich, when the facilities at Harwich became inadequate for handling the increasing number of passengers and there was no room there for further expansion. The passenger terminal was named after the chairman of the Great Eastern Railway, Charles Parkes, when it was opened in 1883. With Britain's entry to the Common Market, the ferry services have gained increasing importance and every year thousands of tourists come from Norway, Denmark, Germany and Holland to enjoy and explore the English countryside. They are fortunate in that they arrive at Parkeston, whose hinterland, the Stour valley, is one of the most beautiful and historic parts of England.

The Harwich to Zeebrugge freight train ferry service which operates from a promontory at the western end of Harwich Quay has an interesting history. During the First World War, the British Government were concerned by delays to goods required by the front line troops caused by the double handling of cargoes at the channel ports. They resolved this difficulty by inaugurating a train ferry service from Southampton and Richborough, at the mouth of another River Stour in Kent, to Dunkirk, Calais and Dieppe in France. Three train ferries were built, designated *Train Ferry No 1*, *Train Ferry No 2* and *Train Ferry No 3*, which were operating a daily service by the end of 1917. After the war the ships were sold by the Government to Great Eastern Ferries Limited who used them to start a freight train ferry service between Harwich and Zeebrugge. The Harwich terminal was opened by Prince George on 24th April, 1924, Prince Leopold of Belgium performing a similar opening ceremony in Belgium.

During the Second World War *Train Ferry No 2* was sunk while attempting to rescue the Highland Division from the beaches at St Valery-en-Caux in 1940 and

Modern cranes designed for the handling of containers at Parkeston Quay.

The Dutch passenger vessel *Koningin Wilhelmina* leaves Parkeston Quay for the Hook of Holland. The Dutch Zeeland Steamship Company has been running services from the Essex port since 1927, and now operates in conjunction with British Rail's Sealink services.

TF3, which had been converted to a Landing Craft Carrier and renamed H.M.S. *Daffodil*, was sunk by a mine. Only *TF1* returned to Harwich at the end of the war to resume freight ferrying duties to the Continent with the name *Essex Ferry*.

Harwich stands at the confluence of the rivers Stour and Orwell, where their waters mingle before meeting the sea together.

> For Stour a daintie flood that duly doth divide
> Fair Suffolk from this shire, upon her other side;
> By Clare first coming in, to Sudbury doth show
> The even course she keeps, when far she doth not flow.
> But Orwell coming in from Ipswich, thinkest that she
> Should stand for it with Stour, and lastly they agree
> Besides all other Roads and Harbours of the East,
> This Harbor where they meet, is reckoned for the best.
>
> *Michael Drayton, written in the reign of Elizabeth I.*

Its association with maritime history goes back to the Dark Ages when King Alfred confronted the Danes here in 885 A.D. *The Anglo-Saxon Chronicle* records the event in these words,

> "The same year sent King Alfred a fleet from Kent into East Anglia. As soon as they came to Stourmouth, there met them sixteen ships of the pirates and they fought with them, took all the ships and slew the men. As they returned homeward with their booty, they met a large fleet of the pirates and fought with them the same day, but the Danes had the victory."

It is believed that the tip of Shotley peninsula, which faces Harwich, was named Bloody Point after this confrontation with the Danes.

Queen Isabella, the wife of Edward II, landed at Harwich in 1326 with her lover Roger Mortimer to commence a military campaign to depose her husband, who was eventually murdered at Berkeley Castle, Gloucestershire. Edward III was only fifteen when he came to the throne but he was soon to establish English supremacy at sea when he defeated the French at the battle of Sluys in 1340. The king assembled his fleet of 200 ships, including nine from Harwich, at the mouth of the Stour before sailing to meet the French. Later, in 1347, Harwich provided fourteen ships and 283 seamen to besiege Calais, which was then to remain in English hands for a hundred years.

The Harwich lifeboat, Trinity House pilot boats and other craft moored in the Pound at Harwich.

Henry VIII visited Harwich in 1543 and had the town's craftsmen drafted to build his warships, *Henry Grâce à Dieu,* known as *Great Harry* launched at Erith, Kent in June, 1514. Henry also founded Trinity House in 1517, and a depot at Harwich services the lightships, which make a pretty picture anchored in the river while they wait their turn for attention.

A Harwich man, Thomas Gray, commanded the Admiral's flagship the *Ark Royal* at the defeat of the Spanish Armada in 1588, while another Harwich man, Christopher Newport, settled the colonists in Virginia in 1607.

The *Mayflower* is generally associated with Plymouth, Devon, but Leonard Weaver in his book *The Harwich Story* presents clearly the evidence established by R. G. Marsden in 1904 that both the ship and its master, Christopher Jones, came from Harwich. He lived at 21 King's Head Street before moving to Rotherhithe in 1611. The *Mayflower* was used prior to its momentous voyage to take cloth to Rochelle and Bordeaux, returning with French wine. Alistair Cooke in his book, *America*, refers to the *Mayflower* as

A plaque on the wall of 21 King's Head Street, Harwich, records that it was the home of Captain Christopher Jones, master of the Mayflower when it made its historic voyage to New England.

being under the command of an old whaling captain. Having landed the Pilgrims at what is now Plymouth, Massachussetts on 21st December 1620, the *Mayflower* returned to England in April the following year to be sold at Rotherhithe for £128. Its timbers, still bearing the name of Harwich, are contained in the famous barn at Jordan's in Buckinghamshire.

Harwich featured prominently in the three wars against the Dutch during the seventeenth century. The First Dutch War, which took place between 1652-1654 in the time of Oliver Cromwell's Commonwealth, was caused at least in part by the Navigation Act of 1651 which forbade the importation of goods to England in foreign ships other than those of the producing country. During the battle of the Gabbard or North Foreland on 2-3 June, 1653, the town became the victualling station for the English ships. Because of the demand for repairs and maintenance to ships the town M.P. Samuel Pepys caused a naval dockyard to be established in the town.

"Harwich is known for being the port where the Packet boats between England and Holland go out and come in," wrote Daniel Defoe in 1724 in his *Journey through the Eastern Counties*. Harwich had been a Packet port from which mail and passengers were transported to and from the Continent since the days of the Hanseatic League in the thirteenth and fourteenth centuries, but a regular postal service was not established until 1661 between Harwich and Helvoetsluis. It was agreed that only English ships would be used, although this was contravened by the Dutch who operated an alternative passenger service. The single fare to the Continent was 6/- (30p) and 12/- (60p) first class, which was later raised to 10/- (50p) and £1 first class when William III introduced a faster and more reliable service in 1694. The packets were often attacked by French privateers, and as a result the packets were heavily armed and if given the opportunity would give chase to the French ships. However, when the new service was introduced by King William strict instructions were given to avoid confrontation whenever possible.

As might be expected the captains of the vessels supplemented their incomes by smuggling, gin, tea and coffee being favourite items. They further added to their income of £10 a month by letting their accommodation to influential passengers, selling food to them and apparently by swindling the Post Office. By all accounts conditions for passengers travelling by packet were inhospitable both on board and in the inns at Harwich where they stayed overnight before starting their journey. Many distinguished people travelled by packet, including the Hanoverian kings, George I and George II, when they visited their homeland. Frederick, Prince of Wales, Princess Charlotte, Boswell and John Wesley were all well-known passengers. Wesley preached on board to the miserable passengers, most of whom would be suffering fom sea sickness, taking as his theme "It is appointed unto men once to die". He probably thought the text most appropriate!

When in 1831 the Post Office accepted an offer from the General Steam Navigation Company to carry the royal mail in their new paddle steamers from Tilbury, it brought the packet service from Harwich to an end. Tilbury at this time was served by a rail link, while the railway did not reach Harwich until 1854.

During the Napoleonic Wars Nelson's fleet anchored in the lee of Landguard Point. Nelson had come to Harwich in 1801 in his ship the *Medusa* to assist in the organisation of a local defence force, the Sea Fencibles, of 414 men to defend the town and also act as a naval reserve. Whilst he was windbound in Harwich harbour he sent out a small boat to take soundings and Graeme Spence later navigated Nelson's frigate through the narrow deep water channel towards the Naze, which Nelson named the Medusa channel after his ship.

Harwich became an important naval base again in the First World War. The mouth of the Stour was jammed with naval vessels of all kinds, cruisers,

Opposite: The tread-wheel crane, probably dating from the middle of the seventeenth century, which was formerly in the Navy Yard at Harwich and now stands on Harwich Green.

Right: A sailing class is towed home at the end of a day's instruction on the Stour estuary.

destroyers, minesweepers and submarines. A local hero at the time was Captain Fryatt, who attempted to ram a German U-boat with the railway vessel *Brussels*, which he commanded. Later in the war when he was captured he was shot by the Germans because of his earlier action against them. After the armistice was signed in November, 1918, a hundred and fifty U-boats sailed in silence into the Stour to surrender, the quietness of their journey contrasting sharply with the previous bustle and activity of the British fleet.

Harwich shipyard, its hey-day long past, continued to work until 1927, when it fell into disuse. During this time it built brigs, barques and schooners, but from 1877 until the First World War it was renowned for the excellent quality of its Thames sailing barges, some of them are still sailing today and take part in the annual barge race past the Harwich yard where they were made. Other fine barges were built by J. and H. Cann in their yard next to the gasworks. Canns used the Navy Yard for repair work during the Second World War.

The Shotley Peninsula divides the incoming tide equally between the estuaries of the Stour and the Orwell. At its tip, Shotley Point, stood until 1976 H.M.S. *Ganges*, the shore establishment which trained junior entrants to the Royal Navy. During its long association, seventy-seven years, with Harwich harbour and the County of Suffolk it won a place of affection and pride within the hearts of the people. It took its name from H.M.S. *Ganges*, the second ship of this name, a three-decker sailing ship built for the Royal Navy and launched from the Bombay dockyard on 10th November, 1821.

Apart from assisting with a naval blockade of the Syrian coast in 1840, which prevented the Egyptians having a go at the crumbling Turkish Empire, and bombarding Beirut in the same campaign, the second *Ganges* served in no other naval action while on active service.

When in 1854 the Navy decided to recruit its sailors instead of relying on the Press Gang to supply its needs, training ships were set up in which new recruits could be properly instructed in seamanship. The introduction of new ideas and techniques, the gradual replacement of sail by steam and the invention of the breech loading gun, meant that skills could no longer simply be handed on from one sailor to the next.

H.M.S. *Ganges* was paid off in 1861 and converted into a training ship for boys at Falmouth. It was an unhappy berth for the ship, with more sickness

Opposite: This view of Holbrook Creek is typical of the scenery on the banks of the estuary.

Right: The figurehead from H.M.S. *Ganges*, a three-decker built in Bombay in 1821.

aboard than on any other training ship, and in bad weather it was impossible to put the boys ashore for their recreational activities. It also failed, understandably, to attract local boys into the navy. Only thirty of the four hundred recruits who joined the *Ganges* at Falmouth lived in the locality, the remainder coming either from London or the Eastern Counties. For these reasons, and the fact that the ship required new moorings and a hospital built ashore, the Admiralty decided to move her round to Harwich. She was towed out of Falmouth harbour on 29th August, 1899, bound for the Stour, and dropped anchor off Harwich, having completed part of the voyage under her own sails. She had stopped on the way at Devonport for a refit.

It was not long before the Admiralty decided to replace their training ships with permanent shore establishments. In 1904 naval instruction based on manning the mast and the unfurling of sails was abolished, making the old sailing hulks redundant. In any case these old ships were impossible to heat, the accommodation was cramped and lit only by candles or oil lamps. It was also suggested at the time that sleeping in hammocks was not beneficial to growing boys as it could cause curvature of the spine.

The site at Shotley chosen for the new base at that time was occupied by two Martello towers, which were built as part of the coast defences from Aldeburgh south through Essex and Kent to Sussex against Napoleon, and a small fort built in 1860, which was still exercising its guns when the *Ganges* arrived in the river. The Martello towers took their name from a particularly strong masonry tower on Cape Mortella in Corsica, which resisted an attack by the navy under Lord Hood in 1794 in a war with France. The towers had thick brick walls with entrances high above the ground and gun platforms on their flat roofs. Down by the river the Marquis of Bristol had just built a pier out into the river next to the *Bristol Arms*, whose landlords had been responsible for ferrying passengers across to Harwich for the past two hundred years.

Upstream from Shotley at Erwarton Hall stands an unusual Tudor gatehouse with semi-circular gables built in 1549. The only other example in Suffolk of such a gatehouse is at Stutton Hall. Behind the gatehouse stands a Tudor mansion to which Henry VIII sailed his yacht to visit Anne Boleyn, whose heart is said to be buried within the walls of Erwarton Church. Anne's aunt had married into the Calthorpe family, who owned the Hall. In much later years the Hall became the official residence of the Captain of *Ganges*.

The shore establishment incorporating the fort and the Martello towers was completed by 1905, when the ship moved its anchorage from Harwich to Shotley pier and the boys marched up Bristol Hill on 4th October to occupy their new quarters. On 5th July the following year the old ship sailed out of the Stour to the training establishment at Chatham, where it remained for a further fourteen years before being broken up at Devonport in 1929. Some of its old timbers were used to build the main staircase at the National Maritime Museum at Greenwich. Two ships, H.M.S. *Caroline* and H.M.S. *Boscawen III*, formerly H.M.S. *Minotaur* and renamed H.M.S. *Ganges II*, remained in the river to assist with the boys' training.

Although physical training in the gymnasium, football and cricket had replaced the rigours of climbing the mast as ways of keeping fit the Admiralty must have regretted the change, because they required boys' training establishments to have a mast to accustom boys to going aloft. The mast-manning ceremony at Shotley, the original purpose of manning the mast being to pay a compliment to a passing ship with VIP's on board, became a *Ganges* tradition and an event looked forward to annually by both the civilian and naval populace. The 143-foot mast erected on the quarterdeck at *Ganges* came from H.M.S. *Cordelia*, a corvette paid off in 1900. The climax of the ceremony came when the Button Boy climbed the rigging to stand on the button of the mast, just eleven inches across and a hundred and forty feet above the ground, and salute.

During the First World War the base hospital at *Ganges*, the first part of the shore base to be opened, was in great demand and all too often the boys were required to form a ceremonial gun-carriage crew to take bodies for burial in the graveyard of the small parish church at Shotley. The victims of a collision between two submarines, the *E4* and the *E41*, in Harwich harbour are

Shelduck over the River Stour against a sky which is reminiscent of a Constable painting.

buried here. In 1922 the old iron ship *Ganges II*, which had served as the base ship for all naval operations at Harwich, was towed away to the breakers' yard. Five years later, The Royal Naval Establishment, Shotley, became officially H.M.S. *Ganges* when it was decided that shore establishments as well as ships should be named. *Ganges* closed its doors to boy entrants in the Second World War to concentrate on the basic training of "Hostilities Only" ratings.

The strong bonds of affection and the high esteem the local people had for the *Ganges* boys culminated in the honour of H.M.S. *Ganges* being granted the Freedom of the County Borough of Ipswich on 27th July, 1971, when they marched through the town with drums beating, bands playing, colours flying and bayonets fixed. Five years later the raising of the school leaving age to sixteen, a more technical but contracting navy in terms of manpower, together with hard economic necessity, resulted in the closure of H.M.S. *Ganges*. It was the longest-serving establishment for the training of young sailors, 150,000 of whom had marched across its parade ground. Its seventy years of service spanned the development from sailing ship to nuclear submarine. Its training methods changed accordingly from the blind obedience expected in the early years to the development of the sailor as an individual possessing confidence, courage and a sense of service.

Almost all of the Suffolk side of the Stour estuary from Shotley to Brantham has been designated an area of outstanding natural beauty, and within it the wide-sweeping Holbrook Bay is a sanctuary for birds. If Munnings found his Arcadia in the Stour meadows, mine must be here, crouched in a small hide with my feet firmly implanted in the mud, peering down the barrel of a 400 mm camera lens at the waders and other estuary birds, Dunlin, Knot, Turnstones, Redshanks, Oyster Catchers, Ringed Plovers, Grey Plovers, and Terns, as they are pushed gently towards the shore by the incoming tide.

Shelducks are another firm favourite and a pair of adults leading between fifty and sixty ducklings of several broods across the mud-flats, constantly threatened by predator gulls, is a touching sight. After breeding in June most of the Shelduck migrate for the summer to Heligoland off the North German coast to moult, leaving their offspring in the care of foster parents. How these are chosen remains a mystery.

The mud-flats in the estuary, once covered with eel grass, are one of the few places where the very rare black-tailed godwits can be seen, while on a warm summer's evening herons coming down to the water's edge from their heronry in Stutton transform the scene into something akin to a tropical paradise.

Presiding over Holbrook Bay are the impressive buildings of the Royal Hospital School, its massive tower a landmark on the skyline for many miles around. It is twenty-five years since I was appointed to the school to teach science and took up residence in this comprehensive boarding school. Entry to the school is restricted to boys whose fathers have served in the Royal Navy or whose fathers are accepted by the Admiralty Board as being genuine seafaring persons, preference being given to those boys who are orphans.

The school is part of Greenwich Hospital, which was founded in 1694 by King William and Queen Mary to provide a home for naval pensioners and for "the education and maintenance of the children of seamen happening to be slain or disabled in such sea service," as it says in the charter drawn up by William and Mary after the battle of La Hogue in 1692. The first ten pupils entered the school in 1712, it then being housed in the Queen's palace at Greenwich. Built by Sir Christopher Wren and his pupil Nicholas Hawksmoor, it became the National Maritime Museum in 1934. Another school, the Royal Naval Asylum, which had had its beginning as a school in Paddington known as The British Endeavour, moved to Greenwich by King George III following Nelson's victory at Trafalgar. In 1825 it was amalgamated with the Hospital school and the combined schools were then known until 1892, when the plural was dropped, as the Royal Hospital Schools. At this time the school was mainly concerned with training boys for a life at sea, and seamanship, navigation and sail-making predominated on the timetable.

It was through the generosity of Mr Gifford Sherman Reade, an East Anglian merchant who owned the large estate beside the river at Holbrook, that the Royal Hospital School came to occupy its present magnificent site on the bank of the river Stour. Mr Reade owned a fleet of tea ships. During the First World War none of these ships was lost by enemy action, and this he attributed to the vigilance of the Royal Navy. In gratitude, he presented in 1921 his estate of 900 acres at Holbrook to the Admiralty, who decided to transfer the Royal Hospital School to new buildings erected on the Holbrook estate. A very fine mosaic in the Lady Chapel at the school is dedicated to the memory of Mr Reade.

In 1943 a committee under the chairmanship of Lord Bruntisfield sat to consider the development of the school in the post war era. They recommended that the requirement of a pledge of eventual naval service by boys entering the school be discontinued, and provision was to be made for a full secondary education, leading to university entry and the Royal Naval College at Dartmouth. These recommendations have been implemented. Boys leaving the school are no longer required to join the navy, although the school remains

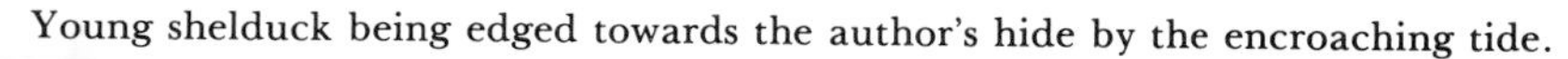
Young shelduck being edged towards the author's hide by the encroaching tide.

A drummer boy at the Royal Hospital School wearing by tradition his dead father's medals when taking part in the Remembrance Day parade.

proud of its naval heritage. Naval uniform is no longer worn for lessons but is retained for ceremonial occasions, including Naval Divisions (parades) which are held on the vast parade ground overlooking the Stour. Colours are still ceremonially raised and lowered just after sunrise and before sunset each day in front of the main entrance.

Boys are entered for the full range of public academic examinations, C.S.E., O level and A level G.C.E., according to their academic abilities and leave the school for further education and occupations in all walks of life, although a Service career remains a first choice for many.

This book has been about our inheritance, in the formation of which the boys of the Royal Hospital School and their fathers before them have played an important part. We, the latest generation of the Stour people, have been fortunate to spend at least some of our lifetime beside the River Stour, which throughout time has flowed through some of the richest pages of our English history in a region of outstanding natural beauty.

APPENDIX I

Fishing on the Stour

by

Len Head

FROM an angler's point of view the river is of the lowland type, with a slow flow, especially in summer. It meanders quietly through agricultural land past the pretty Suffolk villages. At Cavendish the river in the past had been experimentally stocked with trout, and though they never really thrived, a few big crafty old Brown Trout are still present for the angler wily enough to tempt one.

Strictly speaking, the Stour is certainly not a trout stream, for trout need fast well-oxygenated water. Instead it is a river more suited to the coarse fish species, and with these it is well stocked. The present good head of fish is largely due to the efforts of the controlling angling clubs, as pollution has on several occasions severely decimated fish life in the river. The Stour must have a splendid constitution, for it is currently back to perfect condition.

Like all East Anglian streams, it also suffers from abstraction for industrial and domestic use, and the one-time steady flow has reduced to one that, in summer, is barely noticeable in the deeper stretches. Dredging, a ticklish subject with Stour anglers, has also played a part in taking away for-ever some of the river's winding and picturesque character, many of the stretches having been straightened and canalised to aid flood prevention.

The Stour nevertheless is still a wonderful place to spend a few days fishing. Its fish have long held a reputation for being hard to tempt, in fact old hands reckon that if you can catch fish from the Stour you can catch them anywhere! For those that persevere, the rewards can be great in terms of good bags of fish. Species present are roach, dace, perch, bream, tench, carp, rudd, eels, pike, chub, gudgeon, odd trout, and of late zander. A few of the latter found their way into the Stour from the Great Ouse via the Anglian Water Authority's pumping station at Wixoe. Zander, a fierce predator, caused a scare when first discovered in the Stour as anglers feared they might eat up all the resident fish. However, although zander have now bred and multiplied in the river, those fears have not been realised. Mother Nature is probably taking care of the matter.

The most common fish in the Stour is the smallest too, the humble gudgeon, whilst the largest, with the possible exception of the pike, but rarest is the carp, which have been caught in the Stour up to 20 pounds with bigger ones seen but not yet caught. The Stour is, however, justifiably famous for its roach and bream. Specimen roach of two pounds or more can still be taken anywhere between Clare and Flatford, with Sudbury being the best area, and good bags of lesser fish are common throughout the river. Bream, although found only in small numbers in the upstream reaches, are common below Sudbury. This town also provides some of the hotspots for the biggest fish, where shoals of specimen fish are present. At Great Cornard the one-time British record bream was caught weighing 12 lb. 14 oz. Whilst it is unlikely

A quiet stretch of the River Stour at Wormingford.

another as big will be caught, ten-pounders are possible for they are often seen, basking on the water's surface, dangling like the proverbial carrot before the donkey!

Tench, chub and dace are found throughout the Stour in numbers depending on the flow rate. Dace prefer a fast flow and are thus found more in those stretches of river, particularly upstream, where flow is faster. Chub also like fastish water over their backs, but they are a relative newcomer to the Stour and have not yet migrated upstream in very great numbers. Most chub are taken from Brundon and downstream from there.

Tench on the other hand are a slow or still-water species and are most abundant in the slow, deep reaches from Sudbury to Bures and beyond.

Especially fruitful for tench is the old course of the river at Sudbury, where a horseshoe-shaped piece of river was left when the river was straightened. As abstraction increases, so flow depletes; it is thus understandable that tench are increasing in numbers. This is to the anglers' advantage, for they are strong and beautiful fish.

As regards methods of fishing and baits, locals prefer to fish with as light tackle as circumstances and size of the expected quarry allow. Usually float

Len Head with a catch of tench.

tackle is used all through the river, which is trotted down with the gentle flow. Bread, worms and maggots all catch fish, with maggot probably taking more than all the other baits together. During the summer seed baits such as hemp and tares are used with success for the roach. Sweetcorn will tempt many a good tench, as it would carp, though few anglers currently try for these elusive fish. The future of angling on the Stour looks good despite the ever-present possibilities of pollution, dredging and abstraction. Several angling and preservation societies are involved in the welfare of fishing quality, and because they are concerned with aesthetic qualities, too, their diligence can only lead to respect not only for the fish but also for the bankside flora and fauna.

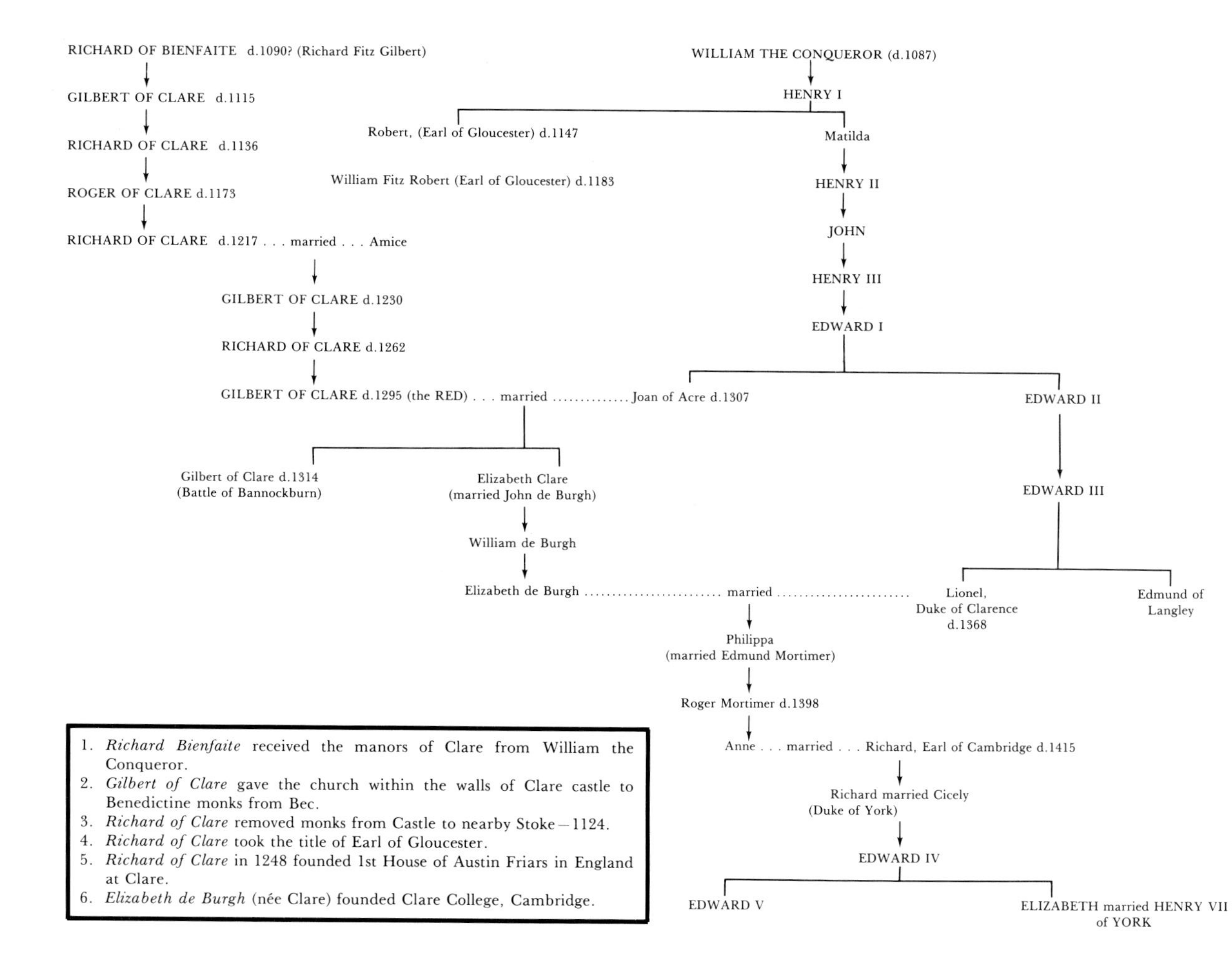

1. *Richard Bienfaite* received the manors of Clare from William the Conqueror.
2. *Gilbert of Clare* gave the church within the walls of Clare castle to Benedictine monks from Bec.
3. *Richard of Clare* removed monks from Castle to nearby Stoke – 1124.
4. *Richard of Clare* took the title of Earl of Gloucester.
5. *Richard of Clare* in 1248 founded 1st House of Austin Friars in England at Clare.
6. *Elizabeth de Burgh* (née Clare) founded Clare College, Cambridge.

Bibliography

GENERAL

R. R. Clarke. *East Anglia,* Thames & Hudson, 1960.
N. Pevsner. *The Buildings of England: Suffolk,* Penguin 2nd Edition, 1974.
N. Pevsner. *The Buildings of England: Essex,* Penguin 2nd Edition, 1974.
A. Mee. *The King's England—Essex,* Hodder and Stoughton.
N. Scarfe. *Essex,* Faber & Faber.
N. Scarfe. *Suffolk,* Faber & Faber.
J. Tennyson. *Suffolk Scene,* Blackie.
N. Lloyd. *A History of English Brickwork.*
F. G. G. Carr. *Sailing Barges,* Conway Maritime Press, 1971.
A. Waller. *The Suffolk Stour,* Norman Adlard, Ipswich.
N. Heard. *Wool—East Anglia's Golden Fleece,* Dalton, Lavenham.
The Victoria Histories of the Counties of England—Suffolk, Volume 2.
W. A. Copinger. *The Manors of Suffolk,* T. Fisher Unwin.
H. Tompkins. *Companion into Suffolk,* Methuen.
D. Defoe. *Tour Through the Eastern Counties,* East Anglian Magazine, 1949.
Philip Morant. *History and Antiquities of Essex.*
J. Pilgrim. *The Cloth Industry in Essex and Suffolk.*
J. S. Hull. *Suffolk Archeology*—The River Stour Navigation Co. 1973.
D. Whitelock. *Suffolk Archeology*—Fact and Fiction about Edmund.

PLACES

Borley	H. Price. *The Most Haunted House in England,* Longmans, 1940.
	H. Price. *The End of Borley Rectory,* Harrap, 1946.
	E. Dingwall. *The Haunting of Borley Rectory,* Society of Psychical Research.
Cavendish	R. Webber. *The Peasants Revolt,* Dalton, 1980.
Chelsworth	G. Pocklington. *Chelsworth: The Story of a Little Suffolk Village,* published by Jones, 1956.
Clare	G. Thornton. *History of Clare.*
	P. Dickinson. *Clare in Suffolk,* R. A. Burn.
Dedham	G. H. Rendall. *Dedham in History.*
	G. H. Rendall. *Dedham, Described and Deciphered.*
	C. A. Jones. *History of Dedham,* C. A. Jones, 1907.
East Bergholt	T. F. Paterson. *East Bergholt in Suffolk,* private circulation, 1923.
Glemsford	K. W. Glass. *A Short History of Glemsford,* K. W. Glass, 1962.
Hadleigh	W. A. B. Jones. *Hadleigh Through the Ages,* East Anglian Magazine.
Harwich	L. Weaver. *The Harwich Story.*
	C. Lloyd. *The Nation & the Navy,* The Cresset Press, 1954.
Holbrook	H. D. T. Turner. *The Royal Hospital School, Greenwich,* Phillimore.
Lavenham	F. L. Ranson. *Lavenham, Suffolk.*
Long Melford	E. Ambrose. *Melford Memories.*
Manningtree	*Our Story—The Parishes of Lawford, Manningtree, Mistley,* W.E.A.
	R. J. Horlock. *Notes from a Mistley man's Log,* Fisher Nautical Press.
	la Rochefoucauld. *A Frenchman in England 1784,* translation by Marchand, C.U.P. 1933.

THE RIVER STOUR

Shotley D. L. Summers. *H.M.S. Ganges.*
Sudbury C. F. D. Sperling. *Hodson's History of the Borough of Sudbury 1896.*
C. G. Grimwood & S. A. Kay. *History of Sudbury,* published by the authors.
Waldingfield Harry Clive. *Beyond Living Memory.*

PEOPLE
J. M. Scott. *Boadicea,* Constable, 1975.
F. Constable. *John Constable,* Dalton, Lavenham.
R. B. Beckett. *John Constable's Discourses,* Suffolk Records Society.
Whitley. *Thomas Gainsborough,* Smith, Elder and Co., 1915.
R. Deacon. *Matthew Hopkins: The Witch Finder General,* Muller.
D. Gibbs & H. Maltby. *The True Story of Maria Marten,* East Anglian Magazine, 1949.
A. J. Munnings. *An Artist's Life,* Museum Press.
The Second Burst, Museum Press.
The Finish, Museum Press.
R. Pound. *The Englishman,* Heinemann.
B. Houghton. *St Edmund King & Martyr,* Dalton, Lavenham.
Lady S. Ryder. *And the Morrow is Theirs,* Burleigh.
Edna Lyall. *In the Golden Days.*

INDUSTRY
J. Merriam. *Pioneering in Plastics,* East Anglian Magazine.
P. Ransome-Wallis. *Train Ferries of Western Europe.* David and Charles.

Index